A TRANSLATOR'S GUIDE
TO SELECTED PSALMS

HELPS FOR TRANSLATORS SERIES

TECHNICAL HELPS:

Old Testament Quotations in the New Testament

Section Headings for the New Testament

Short Bible Reference System

New Testament Index

Orthography Studies

Bible Translations for Popular Use

*The Theory and Practice of Translation

Bible Index

Fauna and Flora of the Bible

Short Index to the Bible

Manuscript Preparation

Marginal Notes for the Old Testament

Marginal Notes for the New Testament

HANDBOOKS:

A Translator's Handbook on Ruth

A Translator's Handbook on the Book of Amos

A Translator's Handbook on the Book of Jonah

A Translator's Handbook on the Gospel of Mark

*A Translator's Handbook on the Gospel of Luke

A Translator's Handbook on the Gospel of John

A Translator's Handbook on the Acts of the Apostles

A Translator's Handbook on Paul's Letter to the Romans

A Translator's Handbook on Paul's Letter to the Galatians

A Translator's Handbook on Paul's Letter to the Philippians

A Translator's Handbook on Paul's Letters to the Colossians and to Philemon

A Translator's Handbook on Paul's Letters to the Thessalonians

A Translator's Handbook on the First Letter from Peter

A Translator's Handbook on the Letters of John

GUIDES:

A Translator's Guide to Selected Psalms

A Translator's Guide to the Gospel of Matthew

A Translator's Guide to the Gospel of Mark

HELPS FOR TRANSLATORS

A TRANSLATOR'S GUIDE

to

SELECTED PSALMS

by

Heber F. Peacock

UNITED BIBLE SOCIETIES

London, New York,
Stuttgart

PRINTED IN THE UNITED STATES OF AMERICA

Books in the series of Helps for Translators
that are marked with an asterisk (*) may best
be ordered from

          United Bible Societies
          D-7000 Stuttgart 80
          Postfach 81 03 40
          West Germany

All other books in the series may best be
ordered from
          American Bible Society
          1865 Broadway
          New York, N.Y. 10023
          U.S.A.

ISBN 1-8267-0299-6

ABS-1981-1,500-CM-08737

CONTENTS

[v]

PREFACE

The United Bible Societies publish exegetical materials in the series of Helps for Translators, and A Translator's Guide to Selected Psalms joins the list of Guides and Handbooks already in print.

The general function of a Guide is to give information about the text in as concise and complete a form as possible, together with suggestions as to possible and appropriate translations. The information is presented in a retrievable form so that the translator can easily find it as he pages through the Guide. By contrast, Handbooks are full-range commentaries that deal with problems of the original text, interpretation, vocabulary analysis, and discourse structure. They also include analyses of translation problems that may occur, and they provide suggestions for dealing with such problems. Both the Guides and the Handbooks are designed to provide the translator with the information he needs so that he can prepare a translation that is faithful to the meaning of the original and has a style that is appropriate for conveying the messsage to the reader in his own language.

This Guide, however, has a special function. Many language communities have never had a complete Old Testament translation, and to engage in such a project usually requires much time and dedicated effort. Therefore national Bible Societies may wish to publish a shorter Old Testament containing significant selections from the various books. In this way, speakers of the language will have some basic material in their hands while waiting for the completion of the entire Old Testament. A Translator's Guide to Selected Psalms discusses psalms which may be included in such a shorter Old Testament.

Other Guides and Handbooks are in preparation, covering material from both the Old and the New Testaments. The UBS Sub-Committee on Translations will welcome any suggestions for making these Helps for Translators more useful and effective.

ABBREVIATIONS USED IN THIS VOLUME

Books of the Bible:

Exo	Exodus
Gen	Genesis
Lev	Leviticus
Matt	Matthew

Translations of the Bible:

NEB	New English Bible
RSV	Revised Standard Version
TEV	Today's English Version

TRANSLATING THE BOOK OF PSALMS

The Psalms are probably the most difficult part of the Old Testament to translate. All poetry in the Old Testament presents problems, but the Psalms have the additional difficulty that they have come down to us without setting or context, for these are often helpful in interpreting other poetic material. We know that the Psalms must have served as the "hymn book" for the Temple and the synagogue, but there are many unanswered questions about when the individual Psalms were used and what they mean.

The translator of the Psalms needs to have some basic understanding of the nature of Hebrew poetry, and in particular of poetic parallelism. He should be aware that in Hebrew poetry two or more lines will often say very similar things, even though quite different words may be used. At other times one line may contrast with an earlier line or express an idea that is just the opposite of the earlier line. If the translator is aware of this, he will refuse to translate words and will look for the underlying ideas that may be expressed in different but parallel language. This means that he will not be fooled by the surface words of a Psalm but will ask about the real message beneath the words.

Whether the translator retains the parallelism of the Hebrew in his translation, with two adjacent lines saying the same thing, will depend entirely on what the function of such repetition would be in the receptor language. In some languages such repetition may be pleasing, even though it is not a poetic device in the language itself. In other languages such repetition will sound childish or absurd. In such a case the translator will have no choice but to combine two parallel lines with a single meaning into one statement. Whether this is done or not, the translator has a major responsibility to do his best to make his translation of the Psalms sound as much like poetry as he can in the receptor language. It would be ideal if the Psalms could be translated into good poetry in the receptor language, but this is often impossible if the meaning of the original is translated accurately. One must simply do the best he can.

One of the problems for the translator is that poetry uses compressed language with many figures, images, and picture words, and this is certainly true of Hebrew poetry. These poetic forms would have been readily understood by those who knew Hebrew and its culture, but they cannot be understood if transferred directly into another language and culture. The translator will often find it necessary to abandon the figure or image and state the meaning in direct and simple language. But then poetry becomes prose. The translator should be fully aware of this problem and be constantly on the alert for ways to build poetic language back into his translation. If, for example, he is not able to retain the language of pouring oil on a person's head with the meaning of appointing him to a task, he may have to translate directly, "he chose him for this task." But when a poetic form is replaced with prose, the translator should be alert to the possibility of translating a direct Hebrew statement in the same passage in a more poetic way in the receptor language. He may, for example, be able in his language to translate a direct "listen to me" with a more poetic "turn your ear to the words I speak." This advice to try to make the translation sound like poetry must at all costs be balanced by the warning that since the meaning of the text is the most important thing of all, the first rule is to make sure that the reader will understand the message!

The translator is advised to begin his work of translating a psalm by reading it in several different versions, such as RSV, NEB, or TEV. This should give him some understanding of the overall structure of the psalm. He should then work carefully through the psalm verse by verse with the different translations and Translator's Helps, including this short Guide. He will probably find it helpful to make notes on difficult problems that have to be solved. He should then begin to translate, keeping before him the RSV, as a base reflecting a rather literal translation of the Hebrew, and the TEV, as a model of how meaning can be achieved in English. He will want to consider the solutions proposed in this Guide on a regular basis, and from time to time he will need to consult other commentaries, Bible dictionaries, and other helps that may be available to him. He should ask himself again and again what his readers will understand by what he has written, and it would be helpful if he had a few average people in mind, so that he could ask himself how would Mr. so-and-so or Mrs. what's-her-name understand this? If the needs of his readers, the requirements of his own language, and the constant search for the meaning of the original are combined under the concern for the leadership of the Spirit, a translation will be provided that can bless many lives.

PSALM 1

SECTION HEADING

True Happiness: "The Righteous Are Happy."

1.1   **Today's English Version**   **Revised Standard Version**

Today's English Version	Revised Standard Version
Happy are those	Blessed is the man
who reject the advice of	who walks not in the counsel
evil men,	of the wicked,
who do not follow the ex-	nor stands in the way of
ample of sinners	sinners,
or join those who have no	nor sits in the seat of
use for God.	scoffers;

Happy: the Hebrew word is used with the sense of "Congratulations," and although the word has frequently been translated as "blessed" (RSV), the meaning is much closer to the idea of "happy," "fortunate."

those who: RSV "the man who," but English more readily uses a plural to speak in general terms. Each language will have its own way of speaking of "any person who," "the people who."

reject the advice of evil men: literally "do (does) not walk in the advice of evil men," but the Hebrew verb "walk" has the sense of "live," "follow," and the meaning is "they do not listen (refuse to listen) to what evil men tell them to do."

do not follow the example of sinners: literally "do not stand in the way of sinners," but "the way of sinners" means "the kind of life sinners live," and "stand" has the sense of "participate in." One might translate "they do not do what sinners do."

sinners: this refers to the same group as "evil men" and "those who have no use for God." It is used in a restricted sense for those who are opposed to God and to righteous people. In some languages a different word may be needed rather than the word "sinners," if the word "sinners" includes all people.

join those who have no use for God: literally "do not sit in the seat of those who scoff (mock)." "Sit in the seat of" means "participate in the deliberations of," "join in the discussions of." One might translate "they do not spend their time with those who reject God."

1.2   **TEV**   **RSV**

TEV	RSV
Instead, they find joy in	but his delight is in the law-
obeying the Law of the	of the LORD,
LORD,	and on his law he meditates
and they study it day and	day and night.
night.	

[3]

Instead: a sharp contrast is drawn between the negative things in verse 1 and the positive things in verse 2. In some languages it may be easier to indicate the contrast in other ways. For example, it would be possible to translate verse 1 "No one is happy who listens to..." Verse 2 could then begin "The person who finds joy in obeying...is happy..."

they find joy in: the Hebrew has "his joy is in" (RSV "his delight is in"), but it is more natural in many languages to use a verbal form, that is, "he enjoys," or "they enjoy" if the plural form is used to express the general meaning of "a person."

in obeying the Law of the LORD: RSV, "in the Law of the LORD," but to find joy in the Law means essentially that it is a joy to obey the Law. A literal translation will not make this clear. The Hebrew word for "Law" means "instruction" and particularly "the instruction that God gives," but in this context that instruction is to be found in written form, probably the Law of Moses (the Law that God gave through Moses).

study: the Hebrew word has the sense of reading to oneself in a low voice and thinking about what has been read; it is sometimes translated as "meditate," but active study is closer to the sense, or "thoughtfully read." One might translate "read and think about."

day and night: "continually," "without ceasing," although, of course, this is an exaggeration.

1.3

TEV	RSV

They are like trees that grow
   beside a stream,
  that bear fruit at the right
   time,
  and whose leaves do not dry
   up.
They succeed in everything
   they do.
	He is like a tree
	   planted by streams of water,
	  that yields its fruit in its
	   season,
	  and its leaf does not wither.
	In all that he does, he pros-
	   pers.

like: the point of comparison is, of course, that as trees prosper when they have plenty of water, so people prosper when they study the Law of the LORD.

grow: RSV "planted," but the emphasis is on the fact that the trees grow there, although the Psalmist may have in mind the idea that just as men plant trees, so God puts people where they can grow. But it may be simpler to translate "that stand" or "that are."

stream: RSV "streams of water," but in English the addition of "of water" is redundant and the use of the singular is more normal. The Hebrew word refers to a man-made water channel or canal, but the emphasis falls on the water and not on the particular form of the stream that brings the water to the tree.

at the right time: "when the time for them to bear fruit comes."

leaves do not dry up: that is, they never suffer from drought.

succeed: the Hebrew verb has the general sense of "turn out well" and should not be understood only in a financial sense.

1.4   TEV
But evil men are not like this
    at all;
they are like straw that the
    wind blows away.

RSV
The wicked are not so,
but are like chaff which the
    wind drives away.

But: the Hebrew does not have a conjunction, but the form makes the
contrasts with the earlier verses emphatic.
evil men: the same Hebrew word as in verse 1.
straw: RSV "chaff," that is, the straw and husks of grain left
after the seed has been removed, but in a non-agricultural situation
it may be more meaningful to speak in general terms of straw.
blows away: the Hebrew verb means "blow away," "scatter."

1.5   TEV
Sinners will be condemned by
    God
and kept apart from God's own
    people.

RSV
Therefore the wicked will not
    stand in the judgment,
nor sinners in the congrega-
    tion of the righteous;

sinners: the Hebrew has "evil man" in the first line, and "sinners"
in the second line (see RSV), but since "evil men" has been used in
verses 1 and 4, language style may prefer to use only "sinners" here.
will be condemned by God: literally "will not stand up in the
judgment" (see RSV), but "judgment" refers to God's judgment, and "will
not stand up" means that they will not be declared innocent but will be
condemned, that is, "God will condemn the sinners," "sinners cannot
endure God's judgment."
kept apart from God's own people: literally "(will not stand) in
the congregation of those who are righteous" (see RSV), but the Hebrew
word "righteous" does not mean primarily "those who are good." It refers
essentially to the idea that they are people who belong to God. Those
who are not able to stand in the congregation of the righteous are,
then, those who are not allowed to participate with God's chosen people,
those excluded from the people who belong to God.

1.6   TEV
The righteous are guided and
    protected by the LORD,
but the evil are on the way
    to their doom.

RSV
for the LORD knows the way of
    the righteous,
but the way of the wicked will
    perish.

guided and protected by the LORD: RSV "the LORD knows the way of,"
but this does not mean simply that the LORD knows where they are going.
Rather, the meaning is that God will go with them along the way, that
is, will take care of. The Hebrew verb translated "know" has a much
broader meaning than the English word, and a literal translation will
not usually convey the correct meaning. One may need to shift to the
active, "the LORD guides and protects" or "...takes care of those who
obey him."

are on their way to doom: the Hebrew has "their way will be destroyed," but this does not mean that the path they are following will
be torn up. Rather, it is a Hebrew way of saying "the path they are
following leads only to one place—destruction," that is, "God will destroy the evil people," "...those who disobey him."

P S A L M   8

SECTION HEADING

God's Glory and Man's Dignity[l]: "God in His Greatness Has Made
Mankind Great."

TEV	RSV
[l]HEBREW TITLE: *A Psalm by David.*	To the choirmaster: according to
	The Gittith. A Psalm of David.

The Hebrew title is found in the footnote of TEV. It indicates
that the Psalm was written by, or collected by, David. In addition it
gives musical direction for the singing of the Psalm, but it is no
longer possible to understand exactly what is meant. The meaning of the
word translated "choirmaster" (RSV) is quite uncertain, and no one
knows the meaning of "gittith." On the whole, it is advisable to follow
the pattern of TEV and put the Hebrew introduction in a note, particularly since the introductions are later additions and not part of the
original text of the Psalms.

8.1 TEV	RSV
O LORD, our Lord,	O LORD, our Lord,
your greatness is seen in	how majestic is thy name in
all the world!	all the earth!
Your praise reaches up to the	Thou whose glory above the
heavens;	heavens is chanted

O LORD, our Lord: the fact that the first LORD is printed in small
caps and the second is not shows that in the Hebrew the first word is
the personal name Yahweh and the second is the word for Lord or Master.
Your greatness is seen in all the world: literally "how mighty
your name in all the world." This is an exclamation and a Hebrew way of
stating something emphatically. The sense, of course, is "your name is
mighty, great." With the addition of "all the world" (which means "all
human beings") the meaning is "everyone in the world knows that you are
great," "...majestic," "...like a king." The translator will need to
find some way to express this idea in an emphatic form.
Your praise reaches up to the heavens: the Hebrew uses a word
(translated "glory" in RSV) that means "height," "majesty," "splendor,"
"power," but it is not quite clear what is said about "your praise," as

[6]

there is considerable uncertainty about the Hebrew text. TEV follows
the interpretation (as RSV) which takes the Hebrew verb as passive,
"is praised." This would give the literal meaning "your majesty is
praised above (or, up to) the heavens," which TEV puts in more direct
English, in which your praise means "people praise you." But it is also
possible to interpret the meaning "you have set your majesty (or, glory)
above the heavens," which may be somewhat more likely. This could be
translated "the brightness of your glory shines brighter than the sky."
Several other interpretations are suggested by the commentaries, but
the translator might do well to use one or the other of the proposed
translations and include the other in a footnote as an alternative. The
Hebrew uses a plural "heavens" to mean what English describes in the
singular "heaven." One may translate "people praise you, and their praise
can be heard in heaven," or "...you hear their praise in heaven."

8.2	TEV	RSV
	it is sung by children and babies.	by the mouth of babes and infants,
	You are safe and secure from all your enemies;	thou hast founded a bulwark because of thy foes,
	you stop anyone who opposes you.	to still the enemy and the avenger.

it is sung by children and babies: that is, "your praise is sung,"
"children and babies sing your praise," "even children and babies sing
praises to you." The Hebrew has literally "out of the mouth of children
and (nursing) infants" (see RSV), but if the line is connected to verse
1, as TEV has done, the sense is clear: "children praise you" (English
doesn't readily speak of children's mouths praising). This is probably
the best way to translate. If one connects the line with the rest of
verse 2, the meaning of the whole verse is uncertain.

You are safe and secure from all your enemies: literally "you
established (laid the foundation of) a fortress (strength) because of
your enemies"; that is, "you have built a fortress to protect you from
your enemies." But it is clear that this is to be understood in a figurative sense. In English it is hard to retain the figure, as RSV shows,
and it may be better to make a direct statement of the meaning "you are
safe and secure..." The connection with the rest of the verse is uncertain.

you stop anyone who opposes you: literally "to bring to a stop
("to still," RSV) an enemy and an avenger (one who takes revenge)," but
the focus is not on one individual. The terms are to be understood in
a general sense as "anyone who is an enemy taking revenge." But it is
not clear what is intended by "taking revenge," and it may make better
sense to speak in general terms as TEV has done.

8.3	TEV	RSV
	When I look at the sky, which you have made,	When I look at thy heavens, the work of thy fingers,
	at the moon and the stars,	the moon and the stars which

which you set in their places—	thou hast established;

the sky: the Hebrew uses the plural (RSV "heavens"; see verse 1) for the place where God dwells and, as here, for the sky, the dome above the earth (see Gen 1.6-7).

which you have made: this translates "your" in the Hebrew "your sky" (that is, "the sky you have made") and "the work of your fingers," but the point is not that God only used his fingers to make the sky; rather, this is a Hebrew way of stating emphatically that God made it, without saying how he made it. In fact, according to Genesis 1.6-7 he made it with his voice.

set in their places: the Hebrew verb has the sense of "fix," "set firmly," but the meaning is that they do not move from their normal course.

8.4

TEV	RSV
what is man, that you think of him; mere man, that you care for him?	what is man that thou art mindful of him, and the son of man that thou dost care for him?

what: after the "when" of verse 3, one would expect the Psalmist to continue with something like "I praise you," but there is a definite break in the construction. In some languages it may be necessary to do more than indicate the break with a dash. One could, for example, translate "when I look..., I think these thoughts: What is man...?" The question is rhetorical, and in many languages a statement will need to be used to express the meaning: "man is so small that there is no reason for you to think about him."

man: although the Hebrew word is used at times of an individual man, here the meaning is "mankind," "human beings," "people."

that you think of him: the Hebrew verb has the meaning of "remember," "think about," "take note of."

mere man: RSV "the son of man," but this is parallel to the first part of the verse and is another way in which the Hebrew can speak of "man." The word mere (not in the Hebrew text) expresses in part what is meant by the rhetorical question: "he is just a man, nothing more than a man, and you should not care for him."

care for: the Hebrew verb is used in a number of senses, but here it has the meaning "be concerned about" or "take care of."

8.5

TEV	RSV
Yet you made him inferior only to yourself;^{m} you crowned him with glory and honor.	Yet thou hast made him little less than God, and dost crown him with glory and honor.

^{m}yourself; or the gods, or the angels.

Yet: this expresses the contrast with verse 4: "in spite of the fact that man is insignificant, you..."

made him inferior only to: literally "made him a little less than," that is, "gave him a position in the order of creation that is only a little less than."

yourself: the Hebrew word (RSV "God") may mean "God," "gods," "angels," "beings that are like God," "heavenly beings." It is not easy to decide how best to translate the word here, but the reference is probably to the heavenly court, that is, the heavenly beings who are associated with God and his reign (see Gen 1.26; 6.2). The translator will probably find it necessary to make a choice and place other possibilities in a footnote, as TEV has done.

you crowned him: "put a crown on him," where "crown" is a symbol of royal authority, and the point is being made that God gave man some of his own glory and honor (see Gen 1.27) so that man as the representative of God should rule over the world. If "crown" is not a symbol of royal or princely authority in the receptor culture, another symbol may be substituted, or it may be necessary to drop the figure and translate "you gave him some of your own glory and honor." It is clear that the "crown" is "glory and honor." If the figure can be retained, one might translate "you gave him glory and honor, like a king who gives a crown to his son."

glory and honor: the Hebrew words are typically used in reference to the manifestation of the presence of God in speaking of his shining brightness and majestic splendor, but the words are also applied to the king. The words themselves may be understood in an external way, "the shining light and the splendor of the royal robes" (of God's presence), but in reality the underlying idea is that man has received a share in God's greatness and majesty. He shares some of God's greatness and majesty in a way that the rest of creation does not.

8.6 TEV	RSV
You appointed him ruler over everything you made; you placed him over all creation:	Thou hast given him dominion over the works of thy hands; thou hast put all things under his feet,

You appointed him ruler over: the Hebrew verb means "cause to rule," and one could translate "you made him ruler over," "you gave him control of" (RSV "dominion over"), but the symbolism of verse 5, which sees man as a king, should be reinforced by the choice of a term for ruling or reigning here.

everything you made: literally "the works of your hands," but as in verse 3, the thought is not so much that God fashioned the world with his hands as that in a figurative way God is described as the creator. Man is described as ruling over God's creation, but of course this applies only to things in this world.

you placed him over all creation: literally "you put everything under his feet," but this is Hebrew figurative language, which is used to speak of a king's superior position over his subjects. A literal translation will not convey this. The Hebrew word "all things," "every-thing," is used to refer to the creation.

8.7

TEV	RSV
sheep and cattle, and the wild animals too;	all sheep and oxen, and also the beasts of the field,

sheep: the Hebrew word refers to all small domesticated animals such as sheep and goats.
cattle: the Hebrew word refers to all large domesticated animals.
the wild animals: literally "animals of the field," but this is the Hebrew term that means "animals that have not been domesticated."

8.8

TEV	RSV
the birds and the fish and the creatures in the seas.	the birds of the air, and the fish of the sea, whatever passes along the paths of the sea.

the birds: literally "birds of the sky," that is, "birds that fly in the sky (air)," but in English and many other languages it is redundant and strange to speak of birds in this way, as it is understood that birds fly and that they fly in the air. The Hebrew makes no distinction between birds of the sky (that fly) and birds of the ground (that don't fly).
the fish: literally "the fish of the sea" as in RSV, but this does not refer to salt water fish only. Rather, it has the meaning "fish which swim in water," but this provides the same problems for translation as "birds of the sky."
the creatures in the seas: literally "whatever passes along the paths of the seas," but this is a figurative way of speaking about animals that swim in the ocean. What is meant are whales, seals, and other sea creatures.

8.9

TEV	RSV
O LORD, our Lord, your greatness is seen in all the world!	O LORD, our Lord, how majestic is thy name in all the earth!

The verse is identical with the first part of verse 1.

PSALM   14

SECTION HEADING

The Wickedness of Men^t: "Everyone Is Sinful."

TEV	RSV
^{t}HEBREW TITLE: *By David*.	To the choirmaster. Of David.

Note that this Psalm is almost the same as Psalm 53. In the Hebrew
introduction (see the TEV note), the name of David occurs, but the meaning is not clear. See the introduction to Psalm 8.

14.1

TEV	RSV
Fools say to themselves,	The fool says in his heart,
"There is no God!"	"There is no God."
They are all corrupt,	They are corrupt, they do
and they have done terrible	abominable deeds,
things;	there is none that does good.
there is no one who does what	
is right.	

Fools: the Hebrew is singular but refers to foolish people in
general, and not to a specific individual (see 1.1). The Hebrew word
does not mean "mentally deranged" but refers to a person who is intel-
lectually and morally not thinking straight. It is used particularly
(as here) for those who disdain God, and could be translated "the god-
less," "those who reject God," "evil men," but it is better to retain
the element of warped thinking if this can be done.

say to themselves: RSV "says in his heart," but this is the Hebrew
way of saying "he thinks," "he says to himself." We are dealing with
secret thoughts and not with public statements.

"There is no God": this is not to be understood as a theoretical
rejection of the existence of God. Rather, it expresses the idea that
"God doesn't do anything," "God doesn't make any difference in our
world," "we don't have to obey God," "there is no God here."

They are all corrupt: the Hebrew verb means "be ruined, spoiled,
no good," and the form used here means "to bring ruin," "to spoil everything," with the sense of acting in a corrupt or ruined way, but "they
have ruined their ways" involves the idea that they themselves are
ruined or corrupt.

they have done terrible things: the Hebrew verb means "be loathed,
detested, hated," and the form used here means "to do things that (good)
people loathe, detest, hate." The reference is to terrible sins and
crimes.

what is right: RSV "good," but this refers to what is good in
relation to God's laws, that is, what God wants.

14.2 TEV	RSV
The LORD looks down from heaven at mankind	The LORD looks down from heaven upon the children of men,
to see if there are any who are wise,	to see if there are any that act wisely,
any who worship him.	that seek after God.

looks down: the Hebrew verb involves looking from a higher place to a lower place. God is on his throne in heaven.

mankind: literally "the sons of man," but this is a Hebrew way of speaking of the human race. See 8.4.

any who are wise: "any who understand, have insight." The word is in contrast with "fool" in verse 1.

any who worship him: literally "anyone who seeks God," but "seek God" is a standard Hebrew way of speaking of worship. In many languages, since the LORD (God) is subject, the pronoun "him" is stylistically more suitable for referring to God as the one whom people worship.

14.3 TEV	RSV
But they have all gone wrong; they are all equally bad.	They have all gone astray, they are all alike corrupt;
Not one of them does what is right,	there is none that does good,
not a single one.	no, not one.

gone wrong: the Hebrew "turned aside" has the sense "turned aside from God's ways," and this is the meaning of RSV "gone astray."

are all equally bad: the Hebrew has the sense "all together they are all morally corrupt." The Hebrew verb is not the same as in verse 1, but the thought is similar.

Not one of them does what is right: this is identical with the expression in verse 1.

not a single one: in Hebrew this is an emphatic restatement. Everyone seems to be acting like a fool who does not recognize the presence of God.

14.4 TEV	RSV
"Don't they know?" asks the LORD.	Have they no knowledge, all the evildoers
"Are all these evildoers ignorant?	who eat up my people as they eat bread,
They live by robbing my people,	and do not call upon the LORD?
and they never pray to me."	

"Don't they know?": In Hebrew the whole verse is a rhetorical question, but it is much easier to understand if it is broken up. If the question will not be understood as a rhetorical question, that is, if the reader will think God is asking for information, it will be better to shift to a statement such as "they don't know anything,"

"they don't understand anything." It is also possible to assume the meaning to be "don't they know that I will punish them?" but this seems less
likely.

asks the LORD: these words are not in the Hebrew text, although it
is perfectly clear that the LORD is speaking in this verse. But if this
is not stated, the modern reader might conclude that the Psalmist is
speaking. It is important to help the reader understand the meaning of
the text.

evildoers: "those who do evil things," that is, the evil people
spoken of since verse 1.

They live by robbing my people: there is some uncertainty about
the Hebrew text, but it probably means "they eat up my people as they
eat bread" (see RSV), which is to be understood in a figurative way,
"they rob and destroy my people as easily as a person eats bread" or
"they rob and destroy my people and this keeps them alive, just as food
(bread) sustains life." In many languages it may be difficult to retain
both figure and meaning, and it will be better to make sure that the
meaning is clear.

never pray to me: the Hebrew verb "call on" is used in the sense of
"pray to." Since the LORD is speaking, it is stylistically better in English to use the pronoun "me" rather than the literal "the LORD."

14.5 | TEV | RSV
| But then they will be ter- | There they shall be in great
| rified, | terror,
| for God is with those who | for God is with the generation
| obey him. | of the righteous.

But then: the Hebrew word often means "There" (RSV), that is,
"right where they are robbing and destroying my people." The word can
also mean "Then," and this meaning fits the context better.

they will be terrified: the Hebrew verb form is emphatic, "tremble
in terror," "be greatly terrified," "be made terribly afraid."

for God is with: "because." The reason for their terror is that
God is with his people, that is, God protects his people and fights for
them.

those who obey him: this is the same group as "my people" in verse
4. The Hebrew, traditionally translated "the generation of the righteous" (RSV), probably means "the class (or group) of the righteous" or
"the assembly of the righteous." The Hebrew word "righteous" means "those
who are right with God," that is, "those who obey God."

14.6 | TEV | RSV
| Evildoers frustrate the plans | You would confound the plans
| of the humble man, | of the poor,
| but the LORD is his | but the LORD is his refuge.
| protection. |

Evildoers: the Hebrew has "You" (RSV), but it is clear that the
evildoers are now being addressed. In English it is very difficult to

have this kind of abrupt shift of the person addressed, and it is much simpler to make the statement in the third person as TEV has done.

frustrate: the Hebrew verb seems to mean "put to shame," but there is considerable uncertainty as to how to interpret the meaning. The most likely interpretation (TEV, RSV, etc.) sees the evildoers confounding and frustrating the plans of good men, or at least trying to. This is then in contrast with the second part of the verse, where God protects good men.

the plans of the humble man: the Hebrew probably is to be understood as "the plans of the humble," although it could be translated "the plans of the poor" (RSV), but often "the poor" are seen as those who are humble and obedient to God. Although the singular is used, the reference is to "humble (poor) people."

protection: literally "a place of refuge," that is, "a place where one is safe"; but the word is used in a figurative way: "the LORD is like a place of refuge for him," meaning "the LORD keeps him safe."

14.7

TEV	RSV
How I pray that victory will come to Israel from Zion. How happy the people of Israel will be when the LORD makes them prosperous again!	O that deliverance for Israel would come out of Zion! When the LORD restores the fortunes of his people, Jacob shall rejoice, Israel shall be glad.

How I pray: the Hebrew has "who shall give?" This is a way of expressing a wish or a prayer. A literal translation will not make this meaning clear and it is better to express the idea directly, as TEV has done. This is also the meaning of the RSV "O that..."

victory: the Hebrew word has a broad meaning of "help," "victory," "deliverance," "salvation," "rescue."

Zion: that is, "Jerusalem," or particularly the Temple, the place of worship in Jerusalem, understood as the point where God meets his people. The prayer is that God will act to save his people.

How happy...will be: this expresses emphatically in English something of the emphasis of the two Hebrew verbs "rejoice" and "be glad" (RSV). There is no need to try to find two words in the receptor language to express this idea of joy.

the people of Israel: literally "Jacob...Israel," as in RSV, but this use is common in Hebrew to express the idea of the whole of Israel.

P S A L M   15

SECTION HEADING

What God Requires[u]: "The Kind of Worshipers God Wants."

| TEV | RSV |
| ᵘHEBREW TITLE: *A psalm by David.* | A Psalm of David. |

The Hebrew title, "A Psalm of (or, collected by) David," is found in the footnote of TEV.

15.1

| TEV | RSV |
| LORD, who may enter your
　　Temple?
Who may worship on Zion,
　　your sacred hill?ᵛ | O LORD, who shall sojourn in
　　thy tent?
Who shall dwell on thy holy
　　hill? |

ᵛSACRED HILL: *See 2.6.*

　　LORD: the small capitals show that the Hebrew was "Yahweh."
　　may enter: the Hebrew verb has the meaning "(enter and) stay." The image behind the verb is that of a foreigner allowed to settle and stay in the land of Israel. The worshiper is seen as a temporary sojourner who has the right to be in the Temple. Since this idea is difficult to translate, it may be necessary to use "enter," for example, "who will be allowed to go in?" "who has the right to go in?"
　　your Temple: the Hebrew has "your tent," but there is clear evidence that the word used for the tent of the Lord's Presence in the wilderness wanderings was used also for the Temple after it was built. The next line makes clear that the Temple is meant, and the reader should not be led to believe that a tent stood on Mount Zion.
　　worship: literally "live," "settle," with some of the same implications as "stay" in the previous line. In fact the two lines mean essentially the same thing. The verb is not to be understood literally, as if there were people actually living in the Temple, but in a figurative way, "be there to participate in worship."
　　Zion, your sacred hill: the Hebrew does not have the name Zion, but that is what is being referred to, and it is a help to the reader to make clear what every reader of the Hebrew text would know. "Sacred" or "holy" means that it has been set apart exclusively for God's use. "Mount Zion" or "the hill of Zion" is the hill in Jerusalem on which the Temple stood, and the word "Zion" is often used as a poetic way of speaking of the Temple. That is clearly what is meant here. See the note in TEV at 2.6.

15.2

| TEV | RSV |
| A person who obeys God in
　　everything
and always does what is
　　right,
whose words are true and
　　sincere, | He who walks blamelessly,
　　and does what is right,
and speaks truth from his
　　heart; |

　　A person: literally "The one who," "He who" (see RSV). The rest of the psalm answers the question posed in the first verse. It may be

[15]

necessary to restructure, for example, "the person God accepts obeys
him in everything..."

obeys God in everything: literally "walks blamelessly," but "walks"
is a figurative way of speaking of living, and to live blamelessly means
to live completely the kind of life that God wants. The use of a verb
like "obey" is frequently the best way to convey the real meaning.

always: the word is not in the Hebrew but the idea is there in the
form of the verb and in the context.

does what is right: that is, "does what God commands." This is
parallel in idea to "walk blamelessly," and in some languages it may be
necessary to express this idea with only one statement instead of two.
It is better to express the idea clearly once than to have two statements
that appear awkward or contrived.

whose words: literally "who speaks." Whether one uses a verb or a
noun will depend on receptor language usage.

sincere: the Hebrew has "in his heart," but this probably does not
have the meaning "to himself" of 14.1, but that what he says comes from
the heart, that is, it is genuine and sincere and is not a lie. In Hebrew
the heart is the center of thought; this person says what he thinks.
Again, if two words cannot readily be found to express "true and sincere,"
a single word that clearly expresses the idea will be fine.

15.3	TEV	RSV
	and who does not slander others.	who does not slander with his tongue,
	He does no wrong to his friends	and does no evil to his friend,
	nor spreads rumors about his neighbors.	nor takes up a reproach against his neighbor;

slander others: the Hebrew verb is related to the word for "foot"
and probably means "slander," "gossip," "tell an untruth about someone."
The Hebrew has literally "slander upon his tongue," but in English
"slander" means speaking, and it seems strange and redundant to state
that the speaking is done with the tongue.

his friends: the Hebrew is singular, "his friend," but this word
has a general meaning and does not mean that the man has only one
friend.

spread rumors: literally "lift up a reproach, taunt, or accusation"
(see RSV), where the Hebrew verb has the sense "talk about," "speak."

15.4	TEV	RSV
	He despises those whom God rejects,	in whose eyes a reprobate is despised,
	but honors those who obey the LORD.	but who honors those who fear the LORD;
	He always does what he promises,	who swears to his own hurt and does not change;
	no matter how much it may cost.

He despises: the Hebrew has a passive construction "in his eyes...
is despised," that is, "he considers...to be despised," but in English
it is much clearer to use an active verb. The verb means "despise,"
"look upon with disfavor," with the sense "has nothing to do with."

those whom God rejects: the Hebrew has "a despised one," sometimes
translated "a reprobate" (RSV), but in this context it seems clear that
the person has been rejected by God. Again, the singular is to be understood in a general way, and the plural conveys this idea more readily in
English. The verb means "refuse," "reject," "despise."

those who obey the LORD: the Hebrew "fear" (RSV) does not here mean
"be afraid of" but "worship," "obey."

He always does what he promises: the meaning of the Hebrew text is
quite uncertain, but this translation understands it in the literal sense,
"he takes an oath...and does not change." The Hebrew "take an oath" has
the sense "make a solemn promise." The person who makes a solemn promise
and does not try to change it or back out of it is the person who always
does what he promises.

no matter how much it may cost: again the Hebrew is uncertain in
meaning, but this translation assumes the literal meaning "to the evil"
and understands this to mean "to his own harm" (see RSV) in the sense
"he takes an oath that might hurt him, but even if it does, he carries
out his promise." This is not necessarily a reference to financial cost,
and one might translate "no matter what the consequences might be for
him."

15.5	TEV	RSV
	He makes loans without charging interest and cannot be bribed to testify against the innocent.	who does not put out his money at interest, and does not take a bribe against the innocent.
	Whoever does these things will always be secure.	He who does these things shall never be moved.

makes loans: this is the sense of the literal "give his money,"
although the idea is expressed negatively (see RSV). In English it is
clearer to make a positive statement.

cannot be bribed: literally "will not take a bribe," but this
refers to a basic integrity and not just to the externals.

to testify against the innocent: the Hebrew has only "against the
innocent" which could mean "to condemn an innocent person" if the man
were a judge. It is more likely that we are dealing with a witness, and
it seems wise to make this clear to the reader. The innocent person is
the one who has not done what he is accused of having done, and the
supposed situation is a trial in a law court.

will always be secure: the Hebrew expresses this negatively "will
never be made to stagger" or "...totter" (RSV "be moved"), but it may
be more emphatic to express this positively. The point is that such a
person has the security that God gives.

19.1

SECTION HEADING

God's Glory in Creation[b]: "The Creation Shows God's Glory."

TEV	RSV
[b]HEBREW TITLE: *A psalm by David.*	To the choirmaster. A Psalm of David.

The Hebrew title, found in part in the note of TEV, has in addition
to the reference to David the musical reference found in Psalms 8 and 14.

19.1 TEV	RSV
How clearly the sky reveals	The heavens are telling the
God's glory!	glory of God;
How plainly it shows what	and the firmament proclaims
he has done!	his handiwork.

How clearly: this is an emphatic English construction that is used
to express the major theme of this section.
   the sky: the Hebrew word may mean "heaven" or "sky," but here it
is clearly the physical world that is in focus, not the dwelling place
of God.
   reveals: literally "tell, relate, proclaim," but if the idea of
the sky speaking is difficult, it may be more meaningful to use "show,"
"reveal," "make known," which involves more activity on the part of the
viewer. But it may be necessary to use a different kind of construction,
for example, "the sky helps us see the greatness of God, just as surely
as if it were speaking." Much will depend on the type of personification
permitted in the receptor language.
   glory: the Hebrew word here relates more to the character and
nature of God than to his appearance. The word means "greatness,"
"majesty," "splendor."
   it: the Hebrew has "the dome," the same word used in Genesis 1.6-7,
but as is shown there, "sky" and "dome" refer to the same thing, and it
may be more meaningful for the reader to use only the more familiar name.
   shows: although a different Hebrew word is used, the meaning is
much as above, "report," "announce," "tell," "relate." The idea of the
sky speaking remains a problem, and a more neutral term is used in TEV.
   what he has done: literally "the work of his hands" (see 8.4) (RSV
"his handiwork"). The whole line says "the sky tells us that God made
it." There is no emphasis on the idea that he made it with his hands
(see Gen 1.3-8).

19.2 TEV	RSV
Each day announces it to the	Day to day pours forth speech,
following day;	and night to night declares
each night repeats it to the	knowledge.
next.	

Each day...to the following day: this is the sense of the "Day to day" (RSV), that is, "one day tells another day." The same applies to night.

announces it: literally "pours out information," but it is assumed that the information is about the glory and greatness of God ("it").

repeats it: literally "announces knowledge," that is, "gives knowledge about God's glory." There may be difficulty in finding four different words to express this idea of speaking, and if so, elements may be combined provided the message remains clear.

19.3	TEV	RSV
	No speech or words are used,	There is no speech, nor are
	no sound is heard;	there words;
		their voice is not heard;

No speech or words are used: the Hebrew has "no speaking and no words," that is, "the sky does not speak any words." It is a bit paradoxical: "the sky speaks without words."

no sound is heard: literally "their (its) voice (or sound) is not heard," that is, "the sky does (or day and night do) not make any noise."

19.4	TEV	RSV
	yet their message^c goes out	yet their voice^k goes out
	to all the world	through all the earth,
	and is heard to the ends of	and their words to the end
	the earth.	of the world.
	God made a home in the sky	
	for the sun;	In them he has set a tent for
		the sun,

^{c}Some ancient translations message;
Hebrew line. ^{k}Gk Jerome Compare Syr: Heb line

yet: the Hebrew does not have this word, but the contrast is clear: in spite of the fact that the sky doesn't make sounds, it get the message across.

their message: this translates two Hebrew words in the first two lines of the verse (RSV "their voice...their words"). The first, often translated "their line," may have the meaning "their call," although some early translations have "their voice," and TEV, RSV, and others assume that this was the original text (see the footnotes). The second means "words" in the sense of "utterance." Rather than try to find two different words, it may be more helpful to combine them into one, as TEV has done.

all the world...ends of the earth: these are parallel ways of speaking of the whole of this world in contrast to the sky. The "ends of the earth" refer to the most distant parts of the world.

God made a home: literally "he put a tent" (see RSV), but there can be no doubt that God is the subject. The sun is part of his creation. "Tent" has the sense "place to stay." The Psalmist is thinking of the place where the sun stays at night. It is thought of as a person coming out of his home in the morning and returning there in the evening.

in the sky: RSV "in them," but this refers to the sky, which is a plural word in Hebrew.

19.5	TEV	RSV

	it comes out in the morning
	  like a happy bridegroom,
	like an athlete eager to run
	  a race.
		which comes forth like a
		  bridegroom leaving his
		  chamber,
		and like a strong man runs
		  its course with joy.

comes out in the morning like a happy bridegroom: literally "he is like a bridegroom coming out of his bridal chamber" (see RSV). The image is of a happy man after his wedding night. This idea is made clear to the English reader by in the morning and happy.

like an athlete eager to run a race: literally "he rejoices as a strong man to run (his) race" or "...course." The word "strong man" is understood in the sense of an athlete, but it may also have the sense of "warrior," "hero."

19.6	TEV	RSV

	It starts at one end of the
	  sky
	and goes across to the
	  other.
	Nothing can hide from its
	  heat.
		Its rising is from the end
		  of the heavens,
		and its circuit to the end
		  of them;
		and there is nothing hid from
		  its heat.

It starts: Hebrew "Its going out" (RSV "Its rising"), but it is simpler to use a finite verb.

at one end of the sky: the thought, of course, is that the sun starts out in the east and ends in the west.

goes across: Hebrew "its turning," "its circuit" (RSV), but again a finite verb makes for easier understanding.

can hide: or "can be hidden."

SECTION HEADING

The Law of the LORD: "The Law Is Glorious."

The last part of the psalm is quite different from the first, and it is generally recognized that two different psalms have been joined together.

19.7	TEV	RSV

	The law of the LORD is
	  perfect;
		The law of the LORD is
		  perfect,

it gives new strength.	reviving the soul;
The commands of the LORD are trustworthy,	the testimony of the LORD is sure,
giving wisdom to those who lack it.	making wise the simple;

The law: the Hebrew word means "teaching," "instruction," and has a larger meaning than "the Law of Moses," but at the same time it is in the Law of Moses that the "teaching" of the Lord is seen. It is thought of as the revelation of the will of God. The translator should make sure that the term that is chosen for "law" is capable of being readily applied to the written law. It may be difficult to find words that will translate the variety of words used in the Hebrew to refer to the law. These are often translated "law, testimony, precepts, commandment, instructions, regulations, etc.," and although some distinctions can be made, the words refer to the same body of law. In some languages only one or two words will adequately convey the idea, and one should use them without trying to manufacture synonyms.

perfect: "blameless," "without fault." The same word is used in 15.2 of a person.

it gives new strength: literally "bring back life (soul)" (RSV "reviving the soul"), where "soul" must be understood as "the life principle," "living." The meaning is: "reading (and obeying) the law gives new life to a person; it makes him stronger," that is, "it gives strength and life."

The commands: the Hebrew word means something like "reminder," but it is just another way of speaking of the law.

trustworthy: the Hebrew verb means "is reliable," "can be trusted," "can be depended upon."

giving wisdom to: the Hebrew verb means "to make wise."

those who lack it: the Hebrew word means "a young, untrained person."

19.8

TEV	RSV
The laws of the LORD are right,	the precepts of the LORD are right,
and those who obey them are happy.	rejoicing the heart;
The commands of the LORD are just	the commandment of the LORD is pure,
and give understanding to the mind.	enlightening the eyes;

The laws: the Hebrew word means "directions," "orders," but the same law is being referred to.

right: the Hebrew word means "straight," "right," "fitting."

those who obey them are happy: literally "making glad the heart" (RSV "rejoicing the heart"), but the point is that the laws (or the Law) cause(s) rejoicing for the person (that is the significance of "heart") who is obedient. This needs to be stated clearly for the reader.

commands: this is not the same Hebrew word as in verse 7, but it still refers to the Law as commandments.

just: the Hebrew word means "pure," "unmixed," "clean," that is, "do not contain any evil."

give understanding to the mind: literally "giving light to (enlightening, RSV) the eyes," but the translator needs to remember that "eyes" are frequently used in Hebrew in a figurative way for "mind," "understanding." The point is this: just as light coming to the eyes makes it possible to see, so God's Law coming to the mind makes it possible to "see" at a deeper level, that is, "understand."

19.9

TEV	RSV
Reverence for the LORD is good; it will continue forever. The judgments of the LORD are just; they are always fair.	the fear of the LORD is clean, enduring for ever; the ordinances of the LORD are true, and righteous altogether.

Reverence for the LORD: Hebrew "the fear of the LORD" (RSV), but as in 15.4, the meaning is not "be afraid of." One might translate "obedience to the LORD," "the worship of the LORD," as well as reverence for the LORD.

good: the Hebrew word means "clean," "pure," "genuine," or in a broader sense "good."

it will continue forever: literally "standing (lasting, RSV enduring) forever." If it is difficult to speak of "reverence lasting forever," perhaps one could translate "it is good to worship the LORD; people will worship him forever."

judgments: the Hebrew word is related to the act of judging, but it has the meaning "legal requirement," that is, "what has been judged (determined) to be the law." It is simply one more way in which the Hebrew speaks of the Law of the LORD.

just: literally "true," that is, "reliable," "trustworthy," "not arbitrary," just. This Hebrew word (different from the word in verse 8) was used in 15.2.

they are always fair: literally "righteous altogether" (RSV), that is, "every one of them is righteous," but the Hebrew has the sense of "what is proper, fitting, just, fair."

19.10

TEV	RSV
They are more desirable than the finest gold; they are sweeter than the purest honey.	More to be desired are they than gold, even much fine gold; sweeter also than honey and drippings of the honeycomb.

more desirable than: "have more attraction," "give more pleasure." The sense is "I (your servant in verse 11) desire them more than..."

the finest gold: the Hebrew has "gold, much fine gold" (see RSV), although it is not quite certain that the second Hebrew word means "fine gold," "pure gold."

sweeter than: this is figurative and has the sense "more pleasant," "more agreeable," "more desirable."

the purest honey: the Hebrew means something like "honey and strained honey from the honeycomb" (see RSV). Since the exact meaning is uncertain and difficult to express, it may be wise to follow the pattern of TEV and combine the two words.

19.11	TEV	RSV
	They give knowledge to me, your servant; I am rewarded for obeying them.	Moreover by them is thy servant warned; in keeping them there is great reward.

They give knowledge: literally "is warned by them" (see RSV), or to state in an active form, "they warn me." But "warn" needs to be understood in the sense of "instruct," "tell how to live," "tell what not to do." This idea is introduced in an emphatic way in the Hebrew.

your servant: this is a frequent way in Hebrew to express the idea of an inferior speaking to a superior, but when used in relationship to God it has the strong meaning "I worship you," "my life belongs to you." In many languages it may be necessary to express this meaning in other terms than that of servant; for example, "your Law guides me in my worship of you," "helps me live my life for you."

I am rewarded: RSV "there is great reward," but in many languages the personal statement is more meaningful, "I am rewarded greatly," "I receive great benefit," or in the active, "they bring me great rewards" or "...benefits."

for obeying them: the Hebrew "keep" has the meaning "obey" when used in reference to laws.

19.12	TEV	RSV
	No one can see his own errors; deliver me, LORD, from hidden faults!	But who can discern his errors? Clear thou me from hidden faults.

No one: the Hebrew has a rhetorical question which expects a negative answer: "Who can see? No one." In many languages it will be necessary to drop the question form and make the meaning clear, as TEV has done.

see: the word is used figuratively, "know," "understand," that is, inner sight is intended, not external sight. The Hebrew verb means "understand," "see," "consider," "notice."

errors: "mistakes," "sins," committed without the person being conscious of having done so.

deliver me: the Hebrew has the meaning "free me," "exempt me," "let me be without guilt," that is, "forgive me," "do not punish me."

hidden faults: literally "things that are hidden," but this means the same thing as "errors," that is, "the mistakes that are hidden from me," "the sins that I don't know about."

19.13	TEV	RSV
	Keep me safe, also, from willful sins; don't let them rule over me. Then I shall be perfect and free from the evil of sin.	Keep back thy servant also from presumptuous sins; let them not have dominion over me! Then I shall be blameless, and innocent of great transgression.

Keep...safe: literally "hold back," "restrain," but of course the sense is "protect," "keep safe."

me: literally "your servant." Most languages cannot use a third person form to speak of the first person. If it is felt important to repeat the idea of servant (see verse 11), one could translate "me, your servant" or "me; I worship you."

also, from willful sins: this is in contrast to verse 12, and the contrast is emphasized by a Hebrew word translated also. Here the deliberate, conscious sins are in focus. These sins one knows about, as they are deliberate choices made by the person.

rule over me: RSV "have dominion over," "become master of me," "make me their slave."

Then: that is, if God forgives unknown sins and keeps the person from deliberate sins.

be perfect: the Hebrew verb means "be complete," "be blameless" (RSV), but the thought is not so much moral perfection as acceptableness to God.

be...free: the imperative of this Hebrew verb is translated "deliver" in verse 12. Here the meaning is "be exempt from," "be without guilt," "be free from."

the evil of sin: literally "great rebellion" (RSV "great transgression"), which is used to describe sin, that is, rebellion against God. The reference is probably not to some great sin, but to the sins referred to in verses 13-14. One might translate "serious sin."

19.14	TEV	RSV
	May my words and my thoughts be acceptable to you, O LORD, my refuge and my redeemer!	Let the words of my mouth and the meditation of my heart be acceptable in thy sight, O LORD, my rock and my redeemer.

May: this introduces a wish or a prayer. In many languages it will be necessary to say "I pray that..."

my words: RSV "the words of my mouth," that is, "what I say."

my thoughts: literally "the thinking (planning, RSV meditation) of my heart," but for the Hebrew the heart is the seat of the thinking process, while this would be called "mind" in English. Since in many

languages thinking does not occur in the heart, it is better to express
the idea in the way this would normally be done in the receptor language.

be acceptable to you: the Hebrew has "be acceptable to your face"
(RSV "be acceptable in thy sight"), but "face" is frequently used in
Hebrew for the person or the presence of the person. The idea is "I pray
that you will be pleased with my words and thoughts."

my refuge: literally "my rock" (RSV), but used figuratively, "you
protect me just as a rock protects those who take shelter behind it,"
that is, "you are my protection."

my redeemer: the Hebrew word is used of the relative who has the
right and responsibility of rescuing, delivering, buying back, or aveng-
ing a person. The sense is "you rescue me from all danger." The emphasis
does not fall on the price paid in buying back or to whom the price was
paid but on the fact of release from previous slavery.

P S A L M   22

SECTION HEADING

A Cry of Anguish and a Song of Praise⁹: "A Cry for Help and a Song
That Praises God."

	TEV	RSV
	⁹HEBREW TITLE: *A psalm by David.*	To the choirmaster: according to The Hind of the Dawn. A Psalm of David.

It would also be possible to use two section headings, as there
are two major themes: "A Man Cries Out for Help" (22.1-21); "A man
Praises God for His Help" (22.22-31). The Hebrew title, in addition to
the reference to David, has the expression found in Psalm 19 and an
expression that probably refers to the tune to which the Psalm was to
be sung. One may follow the example of TEV and retain only the reference
to David in a footnote. It is clear that the psalmist is in great suffering, perhaps from some sickness, and that he has asked the LORD to
help him but no help has yet come. There are many echoes of this Psalm
in the New Testament story of the suffering of Jesus.

22.1	TEV	RSV
	My God, my God, why have you abandoned me? I have cried desperately for help, but still it does not come.	My God, my God, why hast thou forsaken me? Why art thou so far from help-ing me, from the words of my groaning?

My God, my God: the repetition in Hebrew is emphatic and serves to
underline the deepness of the suffering of the psalmist.

   abandoned: the Hebrew verb has the meaning "leave," "leave behind,"
and it here expresses the feeling of the psalmist that God is no longer
with him.
   I have cried desperately for help, but still it does not come: the
Hebrew is quite compressed: "far from my help words of my groaning (roar-
ing)." If one assumes that the question of the first part of the verse
is carried forward, the meaning seems to be "why are you far from help-
ing me (or, from my cry of help), why are you far from my groaning?"
The basic meaning can then perhaps be best expressed by a statement, "I
have cried and groaned praying for help, but you are still far away."
TEV has tried to express this meaning in modern English. RSV has the
same meaning, but it is not as clear.

22.2   TEV   RSV
   During the day I call to you,   O my God, I cry by day, but
      my God,   thou dost not answer;
   but you do not answer;   and by night, but find no
   I call at night,   rest.
   but get no rest.

   During the day: this is probably what is intended by the Hebrew
"day," but the sense is "day after day...night after night." The
psalmist is not speaking of a single day but of an extended period of
time. It is possible to combine the terms: "I call to you for help day
and night, but you do not answer me, you do not help me."
   I call to you: the Hebrew "call" has the sense of "call for help,"
"pray."
   no rest: literally "no peace," "no silence," "no rest" (RSV), that
is, "I am not able to sleep."

22.3   TEV   RSV
   But you are enthroned as the   Yet thou art holy,
      Holy One,   enthroned on the praises of
   the one whom Israel praises.   Israel.

   But you are enthroned as the Holy One: this is almost certainly
what the Hebrew means (literally "but you holy sitting," that is, "you
are sitting on the throne in holiness" or "...as the Holy One"). The
possibility of taking "sitting" with "praise," as RSV has done, seems
far less likely. Although the Hebrew word can mean "sit," in this context it must have the meaning "sit on a throne," with the sense "you
rule as king." If the figure is difficult, one may translate directly,
"you rule (reign) as the Holy King." The But has the sense "even if you
have not answered me, (I still know that you are the Holy King)."
   the one whom Israel praises: this seems to be what is meant by the
literal "the praise(s) of Israel."

22.4   TEV   RSV
   Our ancestors put their   In thee our fathers trusted;

```
         trust in you;                  they trusted, and thou
     they trusted you, and you              didst deliver them.
         saved them.
```

ancestors: literally "fathers" (RSV), but in Hebrew the same word
is used for fathers and for distant ancestors.
saved: "rescued," for example, from slavery in Egypt.

22.5   TEV   RSV
```
They called to you and es-          To thee they cried, and were
    caped from danger;                  saved;
they trusted you and were           in thee they trusted, and
    not disappointed.                   were not disappointed.
```

escaped from danger: this is not the same word as in verse 4, but
the same idea is being expressed. The meaning is not that they escaped
by their own efforts but that the LORD helped them escape.
were not disappointed: this clearly expresses the meaning of the
literal "were not ashamed," the point being that God delivered them
and they had no reason to be ashamed of trusting him.

22.6   TEV   RSV
```
But I am no longer a man; I         But I am a worm, and no man;
    am a worm,                          scorned by men, and despised
despised and scorned by                 by the people.
    everyone!
```

I am a worm: that is, "I am like a worm," "I have lost all the
qualities of manhood and I am like a worm crawling on the ground."
despised and scorned: two Hebrew words are used, but they mean
much the same thing, "disliked, hated, scorned, reviled." It is quite
satisfactory to use one word to express this idea.
everyone: this is the sense of "men...the people" (RSV).

22.7   TEV   RSV
```
All who see me make fun of          All who see me mock at me,
    me;                                 they make mouths at me, they
they stick out their tongues            wag their heads;
    and shake their heads.
```

make fun of: the Hebrew word means "ridicule by mocking, imitating
in a derisive way."
stick out their tongues: literally "stick out the lips," that is,
"use mouth and lips to make a derisive face." RSV has "make mouths at."
If the mouth is not used this way in the receptor culture, some other
derisive gesture might be used.
shake their heads: this is another gesture of derision and mockery.
If the action does not convey this meaning in the receptor culture,
another gesture may be used to convey the meaning or one may state the
meaning directly, "they deride me, mock me."

22.8	TEV	RSV

"You relied on the LORD," they say. "Why doesn't he save you? If the LORD likes you, why doesn't he help you?"	"He committed his cause to the LORD; let him deliver him, let him rescue him, for he delights in him!"

You: often translated "He" (RSV), but from the context it is clear that these words are spoken about or to the psalmist, who speaks of himself as "I." In English it seems more natural to address him as "you." This change of speaker is made clear by they say.

relied on the LORD: the Hebrew text is a command, "rely on," but early translations (see also Matt 27.43) understand it as a past tense, as many translations do today. It would be more accurate to see the words as part of the mockery of the psalmist's enemies, "throw yourself on the LORD," "rely on the LORD." The Hebrew verb means "roll" and is used in the structure "roll your concerns (yourself) on the LORD" to mean "trust yourself (your troubles) to the LORD," that is, "Let the LORD take care of you (your problems)."

Why doesn't he save you?: literally "may he save him (you)" (see RSV), but in English the question carries something of the mocking tone in which the words are said. The translator should find some way to convey the mockery; if necessary, "they said in a mocking way." This applies to the whole verse, of course. The Hebrew verb is the same one as used in verse 4 and refers to being rescued from whatever trouble the psalmist now finds himself in, whether sickness or something else.

the LORD likes you: literally "he takes delight in him," but it needs to be made clear that "he" refers to the LORD and "him" refers to the psalmist.

help: this translates another Hebrew verb that means "rescue," "save" from trouble.

22.9	TEV	RSV

It was you who brought me safely through birth, and when I was a baby, you kept me safe.	Yet thou art he who took me from the womb; thou didst keep me safe upon my mother's breasts.

you: the psalmist is again speaking to God.

brought me safely through birth: literally as in RSV, "took me from the womb," but the process of birth is not so much in focus as the fact that God gave him life. In any case, the fact of birth will need to be expressed in language that is acceptable in all circles in the receptor culture.

when I was a baby: the Hebrew "upon my mother's breasts" (RSV) is a figurative way of speaking of an infant, and a literal translation might be misunderstood. It is clear, for example, that the psalmist is not saying that the LORD kept him safe only during the time he was actually nursing at his mother's breasts. He means that during all his infancy (up to the time he was weaned, at 3 or 4 years of age) the LORD cared for him and still does.

22.10	TEV	RSV

22.10   **TEV**

I have relied on you since
    the day I was born,
and you have always been my
    God.

RSV

Upon thee was I cast from my
    birth,
and since my mother bore me
    thou hast been my God.

    I have relied on you: literally "I was thrown," "I was cast" (see RSV), with the sense "my fate was in your hands," "my destiny depended on you," that is, "you were my only hope," "I had to rely on you." The figure of adoption may lie behind the language, but it is not certain.
    always: literally "from the womb of my mother," but this means "from the time I was born until now."

22.11   **TEV**

Do not stay away from me!
    Trouble is near,
    and there is no one to help.

RSV

Be not far from me,
    for trouble is near
    and there is none to help.

    stay away: literally "be far," but the word is used in the same way as in verse one. The line might well be translated "come and help me."
    Trouble: this refers to the sickness or other problem that the psalmist has been concerned about up till now and which will be symbolized as bulls in verse 12.
    there is no one to help: this means, of course, "there is no one to help unless you help me," "I have no one to help except you."

22.12   **TEV**

Many enemies surround me like
    bulls;
    they are all around me,
    like fierce bulls from the
    land of Bashan.

RSV

Many bulls encompass me,
    strong bulls of Bashan sur-
    round me;

    Many enemies surround me like bulls: the Hebrew has "many bulls surround me" (see RSV). TEV has interpreted "bulls" to be a figurative way of speaking of men who are enemies, and this use is found frequently in the Psalms. It is also possible that "bulls" is used in a figurative way to speak of evil powers, such as sickness. In any case, it should be made clear that the psalmist does not mean literally animals, and the use of a comparison (like bulls) is the simplest way to convey this.
    fierce bulls from the land of Bashan: this refers to the same group as "bulls" in the first line. Bashan was a fertile region east of the Jordan famous for its cattle; bulls from this region would be exceptionally strong and fierce.

22.13   **TEV**

They open their mouths like
    lions,
    roaring and tearing at me.

RSV

they open wide their mouths
    at me,
    like a ravening and roaring
    lion.

open their mouths: not to speak, but to eat up the psalmist.
like lions: the Hebrew is singular, but it is used in a general
way.
tearing: the Hebrew verb is used of wild animals tearing up meat
to eat it.

22.14	TEV	RSV
	My strength is gone, gone like water spilled on the ground. All my bones are out of joint; my heart is like melted wax.	I am poured out like water, and all my bones are out of joint; my heart is like wax, it is melted within my breast;

my strength is gone...spilled on the ground: literally as in RSV,
"I am poured out like water," but this has a figurative meaning, "just
as water is poured out of the ground and lost, so I am wasted, my
strength is gone."
are out of joint: the Hebrew has "are separated," "pulled apart."
my heart is like melted wax: the RSV is a literal translation. This
is not so much a description as a statement of how the psalmist feels in
his sickness; "I feel as if (my bones were out of joint and) my heart had
turned to wax."

22.15	TEV	RSV
	My throat[h] is as dry as dust, and my tongue sticks to the roof of my mouth. You have left me for dead in the dust.	my strength is dried up like a potsherd, and my tongue cleaves to my jaws; thou dost lay me in the dust of death.

[h]*Probable text* throat; *Hebrew*
strength.

my throat: as the TEV note shows, the Hebrew has "my strength"
(RSV), but there is good reason to believe that the original word may
have been "my throat."
dry as dust: the Hebrew has "as a potsherd," "a piece of a broken
dry pot," that is, something completely dried up.
the roof of my mouth: the Hebrew word probably refers to the roof
of the mouth, rather than to the jaws (RSV).
You have left me for dead in the dust: the psalmist addresses the
LORD and assumes that it is the LORD's responsibility that he is near
death. RSV interprets in the same way. Literally "the dust of death."
Others change the text to refer to the enemies, who leave him for dead.

22.16	TEV	RSV
	A gang of evil men is around me;	Yea, dogs are round about me;

like a pack of dogs they
   close in on me;
they tear at[i] my hands and
   feet.

a company of evildoers encircle me;
they have pierced[m] my hands
   and feet—

[i]*Some ancient translations* they tear at; *others* they tie; *Hebrew* like a lion.

[m]Gk Syr Jerome: Heb *like a lion*

A gang of evil men: TEV reverses the order of the Hebrew. The Hebrew begins with "for (because)," which either connects this with verse 15 or is to be understood as an intensive, "truly," "indeed," "yes" (see RSV). TEV and other translations omit it and express the intensive idea in other ways.

around me...close in on me: the two verbs mean "encircle."

dogs: understood as the scavengers of the town or as wild dogs. The evil men are described as dogs.

they tear at: as the TEV note shows, the meaning is uncertain. The standard Hebrew is normally interpreted to mean "as a lion," but this makes little sense in the context, and some Hebrew manuscripts have a verb, which may be interpreted as "dig (tear at)," "tie together," "pierce" (RSV), or some other violent action. The translator must choose one interpretation for the text and should indicate by a note that the meaning is uncertain.

22.17	TEV	RSV

All my bones can be seen.
  My enemies look at me and
    stare.

I can count all my bones—
  they stare and gloat over me;

All my bones can be seen: literally "I count all my bones," but this signifies "I have been stripped naked and I am so thin that I am nothing but skin and bones" (to use an English idiom).

My enemies: literally "they" (RSV), but this refers to the men in verse 16.

22.18	TEV	RSV

They gamble for my clothes
  and divide them among
    themselves.

they divide my garments among
  them,
  and for my raiment they cast
    lots.

They gamble for my clothes: TEV reverses the order of the Hebrew to help clarify that only one action is involved: "they divide my clothes by gambling for them." The Hebrew "throw lots" refers to a form of gambling in which stones or other objects were used in a way similar to the way dice are thrown. The Hebrew has two words for clothes (RSV "garments...raiment"), but only one will be necessary in most languages.

22.19 TEV	RSV
O LORD, don't stay away from me! Come quickly to my rescue!	But thou, O LORD, be not far off! O thou my help, hasten to my aid!

don't stay away from me: the same verb is used as in verse 11.

come quickly to my rescue: literally "my strength, hurry to my help (to help me)," where the LORD is addressed as "the strong one." One might translate "LORD, you are my only strength, hurry and help me."

22.20 TEV	RSV
Save me from the sword; save my life from these dogs.	Deliver my soul from the sword, my life[n] from the power of the dog!

[n]Heb *my only one*

Save me from the sword: that is, "save me from being killed by the sword," where "sword" is probably to be understood in a figurative way as "the power of death" or "violent death." Or, if the image is retained, "save me from the sword of my enemies." One might translate accurately "save me from death." The Hebrew word often translated "my soul" (RSV) has the meaning "my life" or "me."

my life: the Hebrew "my only one" has the meaning "the only life I have," but there is no reason to note the literal form as RSV has done.

from these dogs: literally "from the hand (power) of the dog," but the singular is used in a general way and refers to the dogs of verse 16.

22.21 TEV	RSV
Rescue me from these lions; I am helpless[j] before these wild bulls.	Save me from the mouth of the lion, my afflicted soul[o] from the horns of the wild oxen!
[j]*Some ancient translations* I am helpless; *Hebrew* you answered me.	[o]Gk Syr: Heb *thou hast answered me*

from these lions: literally "from the mouth of the lions," that is, "from being eaten by lions," with reference to verse 13.

I am helpless: as the TEV footnote shows, this represents the wording of some of the ancient translations, more literally translated in RSV, and it may be correct. Others, however, follow the Hebrew "you answered me," which comes at the end of the verse, and take it to be the response to verse 2 and the cry of affliction. It would then be the dramatic cry which separated the first part of the psalm from the second, where one finds only praise.

wild bulls: the Hebrew has "the horns of wild bulls," but the use is still figurative, although in some languages it may be helpful to retain "horns," "power."

22.22	TEV	RSV
	I will tell my people what you have done;	I will tell of thy name to my brethren;
	I will praise you in their assembly:	in the midst of the congregation I will praise thee:

my people: the Hebrew "my brothers" refers to the people of God, and not just immediate relatives.

what you have done: literally "your name," but this stands for the character of the person and is a way of speaking of the saving activity of the LORD.

their assembly: that is, the people of God assembled in worship.

22.23	TEV	RSV
	"Praise him, you servants of the LORD!	You who fear the LORD, praise him!
	Honor him, you descendants of Jacob!	all you sons of Jacob, glorify him,
	Worship him, you people of Israel!	and stand in awe of him, all you sons of Israel!

him: that is, the LORD. In some languages it may be necessary to put the references to the LORD in the same person. (Note "you" in verse 22, "him" in verse 23.)

you servants of the LORD: literally "you who fear the LORD," but "fear" has the meaning "worship," "obey," "serve."

you descendants of Jacob: literally "all the seed of Jacob," but "seed" means "children, grandchildren, etc."

Worship him: literally "fear him" (the same meaning, but not the same word as above), and here since the word is parallel to "praise," "honor," it is best to express the idea in an active way rather than, for example, "stand in awe of."

people of Israel: the Hebrew "all the seed of Israel" has the same meaning as "the seed of Jacob" and refers to God's own people.

22.24	TEV	RSV
	He does not neglect the poor or ignore their suffering;	For he has not despised or abhorred
	he does not turn away from them,	the affliction of the afflicted; and he has not hid his face from him,
	but answers when they call for help."	but has heard, when he cried to him.

He does not neglect...or ignore: literally "he does not think lightly of (despise) and does not detest (hate)."

the poor...their suffering: the Hebrew is a bit difficult to interpret; perhaps it means "the affliction of the poor," but others assume "to answer the poor" or something else. Certainly "the suffering of the poor" or "...of the afflicted" must give the essential meaning.
does not turn away from them: this is the meaning of the literal "does not hide his face from him (them)" (see RSV).
answers: literally "hears," but this has the meaning of "answer a prayer." See "you answered me" in verse 21.

22.25   TEV   RSV
In the full assembly I will   From thee comes my praise in
    praise you for what you   the great congregation;
    have done;   my vows I will pay before
in the presence of those who   those who fear him.
    worship you
I will offer the sacrifices
    I promised.

the full assembly: RSV "the great congregation," that is, "when all the people of Israel are gathered for worship."
I will praise you for what you have done: the literal "from you (comes) my praise" has the sense "what has come from you (what you have done) makes it possible for me to praise you." What God does leads to praise.
worship: Hebrew "fear" (RSV). See verse 23.
I will offer the sacrifices I promised: literally "I will pay my vows," but "vows" refers to the promise that the psalmist had made that he would offer certain sacrifices if the LORD would heal him or help him. To pay the vows required him to make the sacrifices.

22.26   TEV   RSV
The poor will eat as much as   The afflicted[P] shall eat and
    they want;   be satisfied;
those who come to the LORD   those who seek him shall
    will praise him.   praise the LORD!
May they prosper forever!   May your hearts live for ever!

[P]Or poor

The poor will eat as much as they want: this refers to the fellowship offering (see Lev 3.1-17) in which the people (and particularly the poor) ate the meat of the animal that had been sacrificed by having a part of it burned on the altar. The psalmist states that his fellowship offering will include so many animals that everyone will have all the meat to eat that he or she wants.
those who come to the LORD: literally "those who seek him" (RSV), which refers to the worshipers who have come into the Temple, into the presence of the LORD.
May they prosper forever: the standard Hebrew text has "may your heart live forever," but some Hebrew manuscripts and ancient translations

have "their." In either case it refers to the members of the worshiping
community. The word "heart" stands for the person, and this is a way of
wishing prosperity and happiness.

22.27   TEV   RSV
    All nations will remember   All the ends of the earth shall
        the LORD.   remember
    From every part of the   and turn to the LORD;
        world they will turn   and all the families of the
        to him;   nations
    all races will worship him.   shall worship before him.q

                        qGk Syr Jerome: Heb *thee*

    All nations...from every part of the world...all races: the two
Hebrew expressions "all the ends of the earth" and "all families
(tribes) of the nations" mean the same thing.
    remember...turn to...worship: the three Hebrew verbs express the
idea of repentance and adoration, and "remember" has the sense of "call
to mind and acknowledge."
    him: the standard Hebrew has "you," but the reference is clearly
to the LORD, and there seems little reason to explain this by a textual
note as RSV does.

22.28   TEV   RSV
    The LORD is king,   For dominion belongs to the
        and he rules the nations.   LORD,
                                     and he rules over the nations.

    The LORD is king: the Hebrew has "kingship belongs to the LORD"
(see RSV), but it is simpler to express the idea actively, "the LORD
reigns."

22.29   TEV   RSV
    All proud men will bow   Yea, to himr shall all the
        down to him;k   proud of the earth bow
    all mortal men will bow   down;
        down before him.   before him shall bow all
                                         who go down to the dust,
kProbable *text* will bow down to   and he who cannot keep him-
him; *Hebrew* will eat and bow   self alive.
down.

                        rCn: Heb *they have eaten and*

    All proud men: literally, "all the fat ones of the earth," with
"fat ones" here interpreted to mean "proud" (RSV), "prosperous." Many
commentators change the text to read "all those sleeping in the earth,"
meaning "all those who have died and are buried." This would give the
meaning that, in addition to all nations, the dead in the underworld

praise the LORD (see Dan 12.2), but it is more likely that the original text was All proud men.

will bow down to him: the Hebrew has "eat and bow down," but many translations follow a different text, as RSV and TEV have done. This involves no change of consonants and is probably correct, although this is not certain.

all mortal men: the Hebrew, "all those going down to the dust," may mean "all those about to die" (as TEV) or "the dead." The Hebrew has in addition "and he cannot keep himself (his soul) alive" as in RSV (see verse 20), which has the same meaning and may be omitted, unless the repetition is meaningful in the receptor language.

22.30 TEV	RSV
Future generations will serve him; men will speak of the Lord to the coming generation.	Posterity shall serve him; men shall tell of the Lord to the coming generation,

Future generations: the Hebrew "seed" has the sense of "descendants," that is, "future generations" (see verse 23).

coming generation: this is probably what is meant, although this involves a slight change in the Hebrew text.

22.31 TEV	RSV
People not yet born will be told: "The LORD saved his people."	and proclaim his deliverance to a people yet unborn, that he has wrought it.

"The LORD saved his people": this translates the literal "his deliverance (righteous act)...that he did" (RSV retains the words), but "his deliverance" means "the fact that he rescued (saved) his people." Note that TEV has used the more forceful direct discourse rather than saying "will be told that the Lord saved his people."

P S A L M   23

SECTION HEADING

The LORD Our Shepherd*l*: "The Lord Takes Care of Us Like a Shepherd Takes Care of His Sheep."

TEV	RSV
*l*HEBREW TITLE: *A psalm by David.*	A Psalm of David.

TEV has put the Hebrew title into a note.

23.1	TEV	RSV

The LORD is my shepherd;
I have everything I need.

The LORD is my shepherd, I
shall not want;

The LORD is my shepherd: in the Old Testament the LORD is often
spoken of as the shepherd of Israel. One may need to say "the LORD
takes care of me like a shepherd takes care of his sheep" in order to
make sure that the figurative language is understood.

have everything I need: literally "I lack nothing," (RSV) "I shall
not want," "none of my needs is unmet," but it may be much clearer to
express this positively, as TEV has done. The LORD has met all my needs
just as a shepherd meets all the needs of his sheep.

23.2	TEV	RSV

He lets me rest in fields of
green grass
and leads me to quiet pools
of fresh water.

he makes me lie down in green
pastures.
He leads me beside still
waters;[8]

[8]Heb *the waters of rest*

He lets me rest: literally "he causes me to lie down" (see RSV);
this does not mean "he forces me" but rather "he provides the opportu-
nity for me."

quiet pools of fresh water: the Hebrew has "waters of stillness,"
"waters of rest" (RSV note), but a literal translation will not convey
the correct meaning of a good place for sheep to drink without any
danger.

23.3	TEV	RSV

He gives me new strength.
He guides me in the right
paths,
as he has promised.

he restores my soul.[t]
He leads me in paths of
righteousness[u]
for his name's sake.

[t]Or *life*
[u]Or *right paths*

He gives me new strength: literally "he causes my life (my soul)
to return," "he restores my soul" (RSV), but this has the sense "give
me new vitality," "restores my power to live."

the right paths: that is, "paths in which I am safe" or "paths that
lead to what is good." In this context the words do not mean "paths
which lead me to do the right thing," as RSV may be understood to mean.

as he has promised: the Hebrew "on account of his name," "for his
name's sake" (RSV) means "for the sake of his reputation," that is, the
LORD has the reputation of faithfulness, doing what he promises.

23.4 TEV	RSV
Even if I go through the deepest darkness, I will not be afraid, LORD, for you are with me. Your shepherd's rod and staff protect me.	Even though I walk through the valley of the shadow of death,^{v} I fear no evil; for thou art with me; thy rod and thy staff, they comfort me.

^{v}Or *the valley of deep darkness*

the deepest darkness: literally "the valley of darkness," although the Hebrew has been understood as "the valley of the shadow of death" (RSV). But even if "death" is a part of the compound noun, the sense will be "total darkness," "dark as death," and not death itself.

LORD: this is introduced to help the reader make the shift from "the Lord" as third person (verses 1-3) to the second person "you." In some languages it may be necessary to retain the third person throughout, for example, "the LORD is with me...his rod..."

rod: this refers to a kind of club that the shepherd used as a weapon to drive off wild animals.

staff: this refers to a walking stick used for support and as a means of guiding the sheep.

protect me: literally "comfort me" (RSV), but what is referred to is the sense of security that comes from knowing that the LORD is the protector.

23.5 TEV	RSV
You prepare a banquet for me, where all my enemies can see me; you welcome me as an honored guest and fill my cup to the brim.	Thou preparest a table before me in the presence of my enemies; thou anointest my head with oil, my cup overflows.

a banquet: traditionally "a table" (RSV), but to prepare a table really means to put food on it, "you prepare a meal for me." The view of the psalmist shifts from the LORD as a shepherd to the LORD as a host. In some languages it may be necessary to translate "you provide for me in the way a good host prepares a banquet for his guests."

where all my enemies can see me: that is, when my enemies see that you prepare a meal for me, they will know that I am under your protection and they will not dare attack me.

you welcome me as an honored guest: literally "you put olive oil on my head." The good host would greet an honored guest by putting oil on his head (see Luke 7.46), but since this would not be understood by most readers, it is better to express the underlying idea directly.

(you) fill my cup to the brim: literally "my cup is full (overflowing)," but it is clear that the cup has been filled with wine and presented by the host.

23.6 TEV	RSV

I know that your goodness
    and love will be with
    me all my life;
  and your house will be my
    home as long as I live.
	Surely^w goodness and mercy^x
	    shall follow me
	  all the days of my life;
	  and I shall dwell in the house
	    of the LORD
	    for ever.^{y}

^{w}Or *Only*
^{x}Or *kindness*
^{y}Or *as long as I live*

I know that: this expresses more directly the usual "Surely" (RSV), "It is certain that."

your goodness and love will be with me: if treating goodness and love as though they were persons is not acceptable, one may need to translate "you will be good to me and love me." The word "love" here translates a Hebrew word that is very difficult to translate because of its deep meaning. It can mean "faithfulness," "loyalty" (particularly in a covenant relationship), "kindness," "grace," "steadfast love." Here perhaps the element of love is strongest.

your house: that is, the Temple where the psalmist wishes to continue to worship the LORD.

will be my home: this represents the traditional interpretation of the Hebrew "I shall dwell (live)," but the standard Hebrew text has "I shall return" with the sense "I will come back to the Temple to worship as long as I live."

as long as I live: the Hebrew has "length of days" and the meaning is parallel to all my life, "all the days of my life" (RSV), in the first part of the verse. RSV recognizes this in its note, and there is no real justification for translating "for ever."

P S A L M   24

SECTION HEADING

The Great King^m: "The LORD Is King of the World."

TEV	RSV
^{m}HEBREW TITLE: *A psalm by David.*	A Psalm of David.

TEV has placed the Hebrew title in the footnote. Verses 1 and 2 are a hymn; verse 3 gives the questions pilgrims ask as they approach the Temple to worship; verses 4-6 give the answer as to who may enter; and verses 7-10 are a demand that the LORD be admitted to the Temple, perhaps symbolized by bringing in the Covenant Box.

24.1 TEV	RSV
The world and all that is in it belong to the LORD; the earth and all who live on it are his.	The earth is the LORD's and the fulness thereof, the world and those who dwell therein;

and all that is in it: the Hebrew has "its fulness," "the fulness thereof" (RSV), "what fills it," but this is a way of speaking of men, trees, animals, etc., and not, for example, the air as "filling" the whole world. The two lines of the verse say the same thing.

24.2 TEV	RSV
He built it on the deep waters beneath the earth and laid its foundations in the ocean depths.	for he has founded it upon the seas, and established it upon the rivers.

He built it: the Hebrew has a connecting link with verse 1, "because," "for" (RSV). It is the LORD's because he created it. The Hebrew verb means "lay the foundations (of a building)" (RSV "founded it"), but it includes laying the foundation and erecting the building and not just the beginning of the building process. Here the earth is compared to a building.

deep waters beneath the earth...the ocean depths: literally "the seas," "the rivers," but the Hebrew words do not refer to the seven seas and to rivers but to the deep waters beneath the earth, the seas and rivers beneath the earth, the water on which the flat earth rested (see Gen 7.11; Exo 20.4). The two Hebrew words refer to this great body of water beneath the earth, and this will not be understood in a literal translation.

laid its foundations: the Hebrew verb means "set up firmly," "establish" (see RSV). The earth is thought of as being set firmly on pillars which reach down through the underground water.

24.3 TEV	RSV
Who has the right to go up the LORD's hill?[n] Who may enter his holy Temple?	Who shall ascend the hill of the LORD? And who shall stand in his holy place?

[n]THE LORD'S HILL: *The hill in Jerusalem on which the Temple was built.*

Who has the right to go up: the Hebrew "Who shall go up?" has the sense "Who will be allowed to go up?" "Who can go up?" The whole point is that this liturgical exchange outlines the conditions that must be met before one can worship the LORD in the Temple. One might translate "What kind of people will the LORD let go up?" or "What kind of people does the LORD want to go up?"

the LORD's hill: the TEV note makes the meaning clear, and the translator is advised to include such a note or build the meaning into the translation, for example, "the hill where the LORD's Temple stands," "the hill where the LORD is worshiped."

his holy Temple: literally "his holy place," but this means the Temple. One might translate "his holy Temple there," that is, on the hill where he is worshiped.

24.4	TEV	RSV

	Those who are pure in
	    act and in thought,
	who do not worship idols
	or make false promises.
		He who has clean hands and a
		    pure heart,
		who does not lift up his
		    soul to what is false,
		and does not swear deceitfully.

Those who: the Hebrew is singular, but it has a general meaning that is more readily expressed in the plural in English.

pure in act: the Hebrew has "clean of hands," "innocent as far as hands," but hands refer to what a person does and not to hands as objects. The meaning is "who has not done anything wrong."

do not worship idols: the Hebrew "does not lift up his life (mind, RSV soul) to what is false" has the meaning "does not give himself in the worship of idols."

24.5	TEV	RSV

	The LORD will bless them and
	    save them;
	God will declare them in-
	    nocent.
		He will receive blessing from
		    the LORD,
		and vindication from the God
		    of his salvation.

The LORD will bless: in many languages the active form is more meaningful than the literal "receive a blessing from the LORD." The word "bless" is often difficult to translate: "do good things for," "cause to prosper," "do good to," "take care of," "make life rich, or full."

save them: this expresses in verbal form what is meant by "the God of his salvation" (RSV).

declare them innocent: this translates a Hebrew word that means "vindication, righteousness, salvation, prosperity," but here it refers to the fact that God declares the people not guilty.

24.6	TEV	RSV

	Such are the people who come
	    to God,
	who come into the presence
	    of the God of Jacob.
		Such is the generation of
		    those who seek him,
		who seek the face of the
		    God of Jacob.[z] *Selah*

[z]Gk Syr: Heb *thy face, O Jacob*

the people: the Hebrew word is often translated "the generation" (RSV), but it can also mean "people," "kind of people."

come to God: the Hebrew has "seek him" (RSV), but see 22.26.

come into the presence of: literally "look for (not the same verb as in line 1) the face of," but "face" is frequently used for "presence," and the meaning is "go into the Temple to worship."

the God of Jacob: the standard Hebrew text has "your face, Jacob," but some Hebrew manuscripts and ancient translations have "your face, God of Jacob," which is what TEV, RSV, and many other translations follow. At the end of this verse the Hebrew has the word "selah." The word has some musical or liturgical sense, but the meaning is not known. It is best to omit the word from translation, or at most mark its presence by a new paragraph or new stanza of the psalm. There is no reason to transliterate the word. This will not help the reader, and it may prevent him from correctly understanding the text.

24.7 TEV	RSV

Fling wide the gates,
  open the ancient doors,
  and the great king will come
    in.
	Lift up your heads, O gates!
	  and be lifted up, O ancient
	    doors!
	  that the King of glory may
	    come in.

Fling wide the gates: in Hebrew the Temple gates themselves are addressed: "Gates, lift up your heads"; but to speak to gates as if they were persons is not possible in many languages. The exact meaning of the poetic language is not known ("lift up the head" can mean rejoice), but it is clear that the gates are to be opened so that the LORD (the Covenant Box?) can enter, and it is better to express this meaning than to translate literally.

ancient doors: the doors of the Temple, or if the Hebrew word is taken to mean "eternal," the doors of the Temple as representative of "the temple in heaven." The Hebrew word refers to the entrance, the opening itself, rather than to the doors that close the opening, but this idea cannot be retained if a verb "open" is used.

great king: literally "king of glory," that is, "majestic, glorious king."

24.8 TEV	RSV

Who is this great king?
He is the LORD, strong and
    mighty,
  the LORD, victorious in
    battle.
	Who is the King of glory?
	  The LORD, strong and mighty,
	  the LORD, mighty in battle!

strong and mighty: as the next line shows, these words are used of physical power, of the strength needed in war.

victorious in battle: "the mighty one in war," that is, "the one who wins wars."

24.9 TEV	RSV

Fling wide the gates,
  open the ancient doors,
  and the great king will
    come in.
	Lift up your heads, O gates!
	  and be lifted up,^{a} O ancient
	    doors!
	  that the King of glory may
	    come in.

^{a}Gk Syr Jerome Tg Compare verse 7:
Heb *lift up*

The verse should be translated in the same way as verse 7, even though there is a slight textual problem here.

24.10 TEV	RSV

Who is this great king?
  The triumphant LORD—he is
    the great king!
	Who is this King of glory?
	  The LORD of hosts,
	  he is the King of glory! *Selah*

the triumphant LORD: literally "the LORD of armies" (RSV "the LORD of hosts"), picturing the LORD as the leader of the Israelite armies, and perhaps as the leader of the armies of heaven, that is, the angels and powers of heaven. However, this is disputed.

P S A L M   27

SECTION HEADING

A Prayer of Praise^r: "A Song of Faith and a Prayer for Help."

TEV	RSV
^{r}HEBREW TITLE: *By David.*	A Psalm of David.

One might divide the psalm into two sections: "Trust in the LORD" (27.1-6) and "A Cry for Help" (27.7-13). TEV placed the Hebrew title in the margin.

27.1 TEV	RSV

The LORD is my light and
  my salvation;
I will fear no one.
The LORD protects me from
  all danger;
I will never be afraid.
	The LORD is my light and my
	  salvation;
	whom shall I fear?
	The LORD is the stronghold^d
	  of my life;
	of whom shall I be afraid?

^{d}Or *refuge*

The LORD is my light: that is, "he is the source of my light," "he gives me light," where "light," in contrast to darkness, is a symbol of salvation.

my salvation: that is, "he saves me" (from danger, sickness, etc.), "he helps me."

I will fear no one: literally "whom shall I fear?" (RSV), but the rhetorical question expects an answer "no one," and it is often necessary to make a direct statement, rather than try to keep the question when a question may be misunderstood.

protects me from all danger: literally "the fortress of my life," which says in a figurative way, "the LORD protects my life just as a strong fortress protects the life of a soldier," "with him I am as safe as in a fortress."

I will never be afraid: literally "of whom shall I be terrified?" with the same meaning as above, "I will never be afraid of anyone."

27.2

TEV	RSV

When evil men attack me and
    try to kill me,
they stumble and fall.
	When evildoers assail me,
	    uttering slanders against me,*e*
	my adversaries and foes,
	    they shall stumble and fall.

*e*Heb *to eat up my flesh*

evil men: TEV combines three Hebrew words, "evil men," "my enemies," "my adversaries" (RSV "evildoers...adversaries and foes"), all referring to the same group of men.

attack me and try to kill me: the Hebrew has "come against me to eat my flesh." It does not seem likely that "eat my flesh" refers to slander, as RSV interprets it.

stumble and fall: a figure of destruction.

27.3

TEV	RSV

Even if a whole army surrounds
    me,
I will not be afraid;
even if enemies attack me,
I will still trust God.*g*
	Though a host encamp against
	    me,
	my heart shall not fear;
	though war arise against me,
	    yet I will be confident.

*g*still trust God; *or* not lose courage.

surrounds me: literally "set up camp against" (RSV "encamp against me"), "take up battle positions to attack me," probably to be understood in a figurative way.

I: literally "my heart...I" (RSV), but in Hebrew thought this is a way of speaking of the whole person, not just a part of him. "I will not be afraid at all."

enemies attack me: this is the meaning of "war rise against me."

I will still trust God: the Hebrew verb may be understood as "I feel safe, I am confident," but it may also mean "I trust someone," in this case, trusting in God, as TEV has taken it, with the other meaning placed in the margin.

27.4

TEV	RSV
I have asked the LORD for one thing; one thing only do I want: to live in the LORD's house all my life, to marvel there at his goodness, and to ask for his guidance.	One thing have I asked of the LORD, that will I seek after; that I may dwell in the house of the LORD all the days of my life, to behold the beauty of the LORD, and to inquire in his temple.

I want: the Hebrew verb "seek" (RSV "seek after") does not necessarily mean external action; here it is understood as inward aim, desire.

the LORD's house: that is, the Temple.

to marvel...at: the Hebrew has "to look at," but the context makes clear that it is the contemplation of the LORD's goodness that is in focus.

goodness: the Hebrew word means "grace, favor, kindness, goodness," and it is more likely that the quality of the LORD's actions is in focus, rather than his appearance, "beauty" (RSV). One might translate "to experience (each day) how good he is to me."

ask for his guidance: the meaning of the Hebrew verb is not known. If the meaning is "inquire in his temple" (RSV), the sense will be "ask God for guidance and learn (from him) the way I should go."

27.5

TEV	RSV
In times of trouble he will shelter me; he will keep me safe in his Temple and make me secure on a high rock.	For he will hide me in his shelter in the day of trouble; he will conceal me under the cover of his tent, he will set me high upon a rock.

In times of trouble: literally "in the evil day," but in Hebrew "day" is often used for a period of time, and "evil" often has the meaning of "trouble," "difficulty," rather than moral evil.

he will shelter me: the Hebrew has "hide me in his hut" (there is some textual variation), but the words are to be understood in a figurative way.

keep me safe in his Temple: literally "hide me in the secret place of his tent," again figuratively. The word "tent" may have reference to the tent of the LORD's Presence during the wilderness wanderings, but in any case the figurative meaning of protection is to be understood in light of the psalmist's desire to live in the Temple (verse 4).

27.5

    make me secure: the Hebrew has "lift me high" (RSV "set me high"),
but the whole point is that the LORD will protect him by putting him
high on a rock, where he will be safe and secure.

27.6	TEV	RSV
	So I will triumph over my enemies around me. With shouts of joy I will offer sacrifices in his Temple; I will sing, I will praise the LORD.	And now my head shall be lifted up above my enemies round about me; and I will offer in his tent sacrifices with shouts of joy; I will sing and make melody to the LORD.

    I will triumph over my enemies: the Hebrew has "my head is high
above my enemies," which is a figure of victory over them.
    offer sacrifices: the Hebrew refers to the killing of animal
sacrifices.
    his Temple: literally "his tent." See verse 5.

27.7	TEV	RSV
	Hear me, LORD, when I call to you! Be merciful and answer me!	Hear, O LORD, when I cry aloud, be gracious to me and answer me!

    when I call to you: the second part of this psalm is a cry for
help.

27.8	TEV	RSV
	When you said, "Come worship me," I answered, "I will come, LORD."	Thou hast said, "Seek ye my face." My heart says to thee, "Thy face, LORD, do I seek."

    When you said, "Come worship me": there is some textual problem
here. The Hebrew has "to you my heart said seek (plural) my face,"
which is very difficult to interpret. To get the meaning of RSV and
TEV one must assume that "seek my face" is a command ("you said") and
that "to you my heart said" is to be taken as introducing the psalmist's
answer in the last part of the verse. It is very doubtful that the
Hebrew can be understood in this way. It is more likely that the Hebrew
text originally had the wording, "'Come,' my heart has said, 'seek his
face.'" But if the Hebrew text is retained, it is perhaps possible to
interpret "from you (in your name) my heart has commanded: seek my
(God's) face." In any case "seek the Lord's face" will mean "worship
Him," "come into his presence." One might translate the verse "I remember your command; you said, 'Come to me.' Therefore I seek your
presence, Lord."

27.9	TEV	RSV

TEV

Don't hide yourself from
    me!

Don't be angry with me;
    don't turn your servant
    away.
You have been my help;
    don't leave me, don't
    abandon me,
    O God, my savior.

RSV

Hide not thy face from me.

Turn not thy servant away in
    anger,
    thou who hast been my help.
Cast me not off, forsake me
    not,
    O God of my salvation!

Don't hide yourself: the literal "don't hide your face" is a
figurative way of saying "don't reject me," "don't turn away from me,"
"don't be angry with me."
    Don't be angry with me; don't turn your servant away: literally
"don't turn away your servant in anger," but "your servant" means "me,
your servant" (see 19.11), "the one who has served you." The sense is
"I have worshiped you, don't now be angry and abandon me," as in the
last part of the verse.
    God, my savior: the Hebrew "God of my salvation" (RSV) means "God
who saves me."

27.10	TEV	RSV

TEV

My father and mother may
    abandon me,
but the LORD will take
    care of me.

RSV

For my father and my mother
    have forsaken me,
but the LORD will take me
    up.

may abandon me: this expresses a kind of condition, "if my parents
abandon me, the LORD will..." This is a more likely interpretation of
the Hebrew than the RSV "For...have forsaken."
    take care of me: literally "will take me in" (as one takes in an
orphan), but the meaning is "care for me." RSV "take me up" has the
same meaning.

27.11	TEV	RSV

TEV

Teach me, LORD, what you want
    me to do,
and lead me along a safe
    path,
    because I have many enemies.

RSV

Teach me thy way, O LORD;
    and lead me on a level
    path
    because of my enemies.

what you want me to do: the Hebrew "your way" (see RSV) does not
mean "the path you walk"; it means "the path you want me to walk in,"
and it is a figure for "the kind of life you want me to live."
    safe path: the Hebrew "a level path" (RSV) probably means "a path
that is not dangerous."
    because I have many enemies: that is the meaning of "because of my
enemies" (RSV), that is, "because my enemies attack me."

27.12 TEV	RSV
Don't abandon me to my enemies, who attack me with lies and threats.	Give me not up to the will of my adversaries; for false witnesses have risen against me, and they breathe out violence.

Don't abandon me to my enemies: the Hebrew has "don't give me to the soul (will) of my enemies," and as noted earlier, the word often translated "soul" has many other meanings. Here the word refers to the person as willing or desiring. The sense is "don't let the desire (will) of my enemies (what my enemies want) be done to me."

attack me with lies: the Hebrew "lying witnesses rise against me" refers to enemies who stand (in court) to make false accusations against the psalmist.

threats: the Hebrew text is not clear, but it seems to mean "a witness of violence," but others understand the text to mean "they breathe out violence" (RSV). In any case, the sense will be "they threaten me."

27.13 TEV	RSV
I know that I will live to see the LORD's goodness in this present life.	I believe that I shall see the goodness of the LORD in the land of the living!

the LORD's goodness: although a different Hebrew word is used, the idea is similar to that expressed in verse 4.

in this present life: this is the meaning of the literal "in the land of the living" (RSV).

27.14 TEV	RSV
Trust in the LORD. Have faith, do not despair. Trust in the LORD.	Wait for the LORD; be strong, and let your heart take courage; yea, wait for the LORD!

Trust in: the Hebrew "Wait for" (RSV) has the sense of "expect him to act," "trust him."

Have faith: the Hebrew "be strong" (RSV) is used with the sense "be courageous," "be confident."

do not despair: the Hebrew "let your heart be strong," has the sense of "be courageous." RSV has retained "heart," but in English one normally speaks of the person (and this is what "heart" means here) being courageous.

PSALM   32

SECTION HEADING

Confession and Forgiveness[b]: "God Forgives a Sinner Who Repents."

TEV	RSV
[b]HEBREW TITLE: *A poem by David.*	A Psalm of David. A Maskil.

TEV has put the Hebrew title in the footnote.

<table>
<tr><td>32.1</td><td align="center">TEV</td><td align="center">RSV</td></tr>
</table>

TEV	RSV
Happy are those whose sins	Blessed is he whose trans-
are forgiven,	gression is forgiven,
whose wrongs are pardoned.	whose sin is covered.

Happy: the Hebrew word has the sense of "fortunate," "in a favored situation," "to be congratulated."

are those: in the Hebrew the singular is used to refer to people in general.

sins: the Hebrew word has the meaning of rebellion or disobedience against the will of God (RSV "transgression"), but no sharp distinction can be drawn between this and the following words for sin. It may be necessary to use the same word for sin in translation, even when the Hebrew may have different words.

wrongs: "misconduct," "wrong-doing," "sin" (RSV).

forgiven...pardoned: literally "lifted up...covered" (see RSV), but the words are used in a figurative way for the fact that sins are no longer a barrier between the sinner and God.

| 32.1   TEV | RSV |

32.2 TEV	RSV
Happy is the man whom the	Blessed is the man to whom
LORD does not accuse	the LORD imputes no
of doing wrong	iniquity,
and who is free from all	and in whose spirit there
deceit.	is no deceit.

does not accuse: the Hebrew "does not consider (reckon)" (RSV "imputes no") is a declaration of innocence, and one might translate "declares to be innocent."

wrong: another Hebrew word for sin, which emphasizes its crooked-ness, wrongness (RSV "iniquity").

is free from: literally "there is not in his spirit" (as in RSV), but the word "spirit," like the words "soul," "heart," often means the person himself, that is, "there is not in him."

deceit: "falsehood," "attempt to conceal."

32.3 TEV	RSV
When I did not confess my sins, I was worn out from crying all day long.	When I declared not my sin, my body wasted away through my groaning all day long.

did not confess: literally "kept still," that is, "did not speak to acknowledge my sin." Note RSV "declared not."

I was worn out: the Hebrew has "my bones were worn out" or "my bones wasted away" (see RSV), but "bones" is frequently used in a figurative way for "body." One could translate "my body was worn out," but it is more natural in English to say "I was exhausted" or "...finished." It is also possible to restructure, "I was so sick that I cried from morning to night."

crying: "groaning" (RSV), "moaning" in prayer for help. See 22.2.

32.4 TEV	RSV
Day and night you punished me, LORD; my strength was completely drained, as moisture is dried up by the summer heat.	For day and night thy hand was heavy upon me; my strength was dried up[o] as by the heat of summer. *Selah*

[o]Heb obscure

you punished me: that is what is meant by the literal "your hand was heavy upon me" (RSV).

my strength was completely drained: the meaning of the Hebrew is uncertain. TEV assumes a literal text, "my moisture (my strength) was dried up," as does RSV. Others make a textual change to "my heart failed," "my tongue was changed," or something else.

as moisture is dried up by the summer heat: the Hebrew has "in (some manuscripts: as) the dry heat of summer," but the meaning will depend on the previous line. See 24.6 for the Hebrew ending of the verse.

32.5 TEV	RSV
Then I confessed my sins to you; I did not conceal my wrong-doings. I decided to confess them to you, and you forgave all my sins.	I acknowledged my sin to thee, and I did not hide my iniquity; I said, "I will confess my transgressions to the LORD"; then thou didst forgive the guilt of my sin. *Selah*

I confessed...to you: literally, "I caused you to know," that is, "I told you."

did not conceal: the Hebrew has "did not cover" (RSV "did not hide"), but here in a different sense from "pardon" in verse 1.

I decided to confess them to you: RSV preserves the more literal "I said 'I will confess my sins to the LORD,'" but TEV has shifted to indirect discourse.

all my sins: RSV retains the more literal "the guilt (or penalty) of my sin." See 24.6 for the Hebrew ending of the verse.

32.6 TEV	RSV
So all your loyal people should pray to you in times of need;c when a great flood of trouble comes rushing in, it will not reach them.	Therefore let every one who is godly offer prayer to thee; at a time of distress,P in the rush of great waters, they shall not reach him.

cSome ancient translations need; Hebrew finding only.   PCn: Heb at a time of finding only

So: "therefore," "because of this," that is, "because the Lord forgives sins."

all your loyal people: the Hebrew word means "faithful," "loyal," "fulfilling ones obligations," which RSV translates as "godly." The Hebrew uses the singular in a general way.

in times of need: the Hebrew text is unclear, "in a time of finding only." Many translations change the text, as RSV and TEV have done, to mean "in time of hardship" or "in a time of trouble." Some, however, try to retain the Hebrew text with the sense "at a time when (a person) discovers (his sin) only" or "at a time when (a person) finds himself (in the presence of the LORD) only," but this is certainly very unusual Hebrew.

when a great flood of trouble comes rushing in: literally "in a flood of great waters" (see RSV), which is interpreted in a figurative way, as elsewhere in the Old Testament.

32.7 TEV	RSV
You are my hiding place; you will save me from trouble. I sing aloud of your salvation, because you protect me.	Thou art a hiding place for me, thou preservest me from trouble; thou dost encompass me with deliverance.q Selah

qCn: Heb shouts of deliverance

my hiding place: that is, "in your presence I am as safe as if I were hidden from my enemies" or "...from danger."

save: "guard," "protect," "keep."

I sing aloud of your salvation, because you protect me: the Hebrew is unclear, perhaps "shouts to deliver (protect), you surround me," which possibly means "you surround me with people who shout to encourage

me about my deliverance" or "...to rejoice with me in my deliverance."
Others, such as RSV, drop the word for "shouts" or change the text in
other ways. At best, the meaning of the text is uncertain.

32.8	TEV	RSV
	The LORD says, "I will teach you the way you should go; I will instruct you and advise you.	I will instruct you and teach you the way you should go; I will counsel you with my eye upon you.

The LORD says: these words are not in the text, but the translator
needs to help his reader understand that the "I" of the verse is not the
psalmist, as some may take it.
    advise you: the literal "my eye upon you" (RSV) has the sense, "I
will direct you," "take care of you."

32.9	TEV	RSV
	Don't be stupid like a horse or a mule, which must be controlled with a bit and bridle to make it submit."	Be not like a horse or a mule, without understanding, which must be curbed with bit and bridle, else it will not keep with you.

stupid: "without understanding or discernment."
bit: the metal part of the bridle (harness) that is inserted into
the mouth of an animal and used to control it.
    to make it submit: there is much uncertainty about the meaning of
the Hebrew in this part of the verse. The Hebrew "not near you" is interpreted "otherwise it will not obey you" (see RSV "else it will not
keep with you"), but there are a number of other possibilities. About
the best the translator can do is follow a meaningful translation like
TEV.

32.10	TEV	RSV
	The wicked will have to suffer, but those who trust in the LORD are protected by his constant love.	Many are the pangs of the wicked; but steadfast love surrounds him who trusts in the LORD.

.   The wicked will have to suffer: the Hebrew has "many the pains
(sufferings) to the wicked men" (note RSV), but the singular is used in
a general sense.
    are protected: literally "are surrounded," but that is for pro-
tection. RSV has shifted to the active voice, "surrounds him."
    constant love: the Hebrew word involves "love," "faithfulness,"
"loyalty," "kindness."

32.11	TEV		RSV

32.11 TEV
You that are righteous, be
   glad and rejoice
because of what the LORD
   has done.
You that obey him, shout
   for joy!

RSV
Be glad in the LORD, and
   rejoice, O righteous,
and shout for joy, all you
   upright in heart!

because of what the LORD has done: literally "in the LORD" (RSV),
but this is taken to mean "in what the LORD is and what he has done."
   You that obey him: literally "all the upright (straight) in
heart," but these are the people who obey God's commands.

P S A L M S   42-43

SECTION HEADING

   The Prayer of a Man in Exileᵠ: "A Man Far From Home Prays to God."

TEV
ᵠHEBREW TITLE: *A poem by the clan
of Korah.*

RSV
To the choirmaster: A Maskil of the
Sons of Korah.

   It is generally recognized that Psalms 42 and 43 belong together as
a single Psalm. Note the refrain in 42.5-11; 43.5. TEV has placed the
Hebrew title in the footnote.

42.1 TEV
As a deer longs for a stream
   of cool water,
so I long for you, O God.

RSV
As a hart longs
for flowing streams
so longs my soul
   for thee, O God.

   deer: there is no need to try to be specific in identifying the
particular kind of deer that lived in Palestine. The psalmist compares
his longing for the Temple with the animal's desire for water.
   a stream of cool water: literally "streams of water."
   I: in Hebrew "my soul" (RSV) is used frequently for the person.

42.2 TEV
I thirst for you, the living
   God.
When can I go and worship
   in your presence?

RSV
My soul thirsts for God,
   for the living God.
When shall I come and
   behold
   the face of God?

thirst: used figuratively for deep longing and desire.

worship in your presence: the Hebrew has "see the face of God" (see RSV), but "seek the face" or "see the face" means worship in the Temple. See 24.6; 27.8.

42.3	TEV	RSV
	Day and night I cry, 　and tears are my only food; all the time my enemies ask 　me, "Where is your God?"	My tears have been my food 　day and night, while men say to me con- 　　tinually, "Where is your God?"

I cry, and tears are my only food: literally "my tears are to me food" (see RSV), but many readers will need help to understand what this means: "I cry day and night and eat nothing."

my enemies: the subject is not expressed in the Hebrew (RSV supplies "men"), but these people are obviously enemies, and possibly not Jews, since "Where is your God?" is natural on the lips of non-Jews. Their question is rhetorical and means "Your God doesn't exist."

42.4	TEV	RSV
	My heart breaks when I 　remember the past, when I went with the crowds 　to the house of God and led them as they walked 　along, a happy crowd, singing and 　shouting praise to God.	These things I remember, 　as I pour out my soul: how I went with the throng, 　and led them in procession 　　to the house of God, with glad shouts and songs 　of thanksgiving, a multitude keeping festival.

My heart breaks: literally "I pour out upon me (within me) my soul (life)," either in mourning (TEV) or in giving full expression to his feelings. RSV retains the form, but the meaning is not clear.

with the crowds: the meaning of the Hebrew is not known with any certainty, but the meaning may be "under the tent," a reference to a covered shelter leading to the Temple.

and led them as they walked along: the meaning of the Hebrew is not known with certainty. Others take the meaning to be (combined with the previous word): "into the tent of the Glorious One (the Lord)."

happy crowd: RSV "a multitude keeping festival." It is clear that this part of the verse reflects the joy of pilgrims going to the Temple.

42.5	TEV	RSV
	Why am I so sad? 　Why am I so troubled? I will put my hope in God, 　and once again I will praise 　him, my savior and my God.	Why are you cast down, O my 　soul, 　and why are you disquieted 　within me? Hope in God; for I shall 　again praise him, my help 6 and my God.

Why am I so sad?: literally "why are you bowed down, my soul" (see RSV), but this is a figurative way of speaking of one's sadness.

troubled: literally "groan," but in the sense of expressing sadness, trouble, worry. Note RSV "disquieted."

I will put my hope: in English it is easier to express this idea as a strong promise than it is to use a command to oneself, as in RSV.

my savior and my God: the Hebrew text is awkward here, but TEV assumes that the original text was the same as in verse 12 and 43.5, literally "the salvation of my face (me) and my God," that is, "my God who saves me." RSV translates all three as "my help and my God." In the Hebrew text verse 6 begins with "(and) my God," as in RSV.

42.6-7 TEV	RSV
Here in exile my heart is breaking, and so I turn my thoughts to him. He has sent waves of sorrow over my soul; chaos roars at me like a flood, like waterfalls thundering down to the Jordan from Mount Hermon and Mount Mizar.	My soul is cast down within me, therefore I remember thee from the land of Jordan and of Hermon, from Mount Mizar. 7 Deep calls to deep at the thunder of thy cataracts; all thy waves and thy billows have gone over me.

Here in exile: these words are not in the Hebrew text, but the context makes clear that this is the situation. If it is not stated explicitly, many readers will not understand what is meant. The order of verse elements has been changed in TEV so that it will be clear that the geographical references are to be taken with what follows, and not with "I turn my thoughts to you."

my heart is breaking: literally "my soul is melted (or bowed down) upon me," but this is a figurative way of speaking of grief and sorrow, here because of his absence from Jerusalem.

He has sent waves of sorrow over my soul: TEV has interpreted the references to the sea as figurative expressions of great sorrow; the forces of chaos overwhelm the psalmist. The Hebrew has "deep (the depths of chaos) calls to deep at the voice of your water spouts (cataracts) (the meaning of the Hebrew word is uncertain), all your breakers and waves have passed over me" (see RSV). The psalmist describes himself as drowning in the sea, but this is probably figurative.

from Mount Hermon: literally "from the land of Jordan (the sources of the Jordan River in Mount Hermon) and Hermon," referring to Mount Hermon (75 kilometers, or 46 miles, northeast of Lake Galilee), where Jordan starts.

and Mount Mizar: possibly a smaller peak in the Mount Hermon area, but not known with certainty.

	TEV	RSV
42.8	May the LORD show his constant love during the day, so that I may have a song at night, a prayer to the God of my life.	By day the LORD commands his steadfast love; and at night his song is with me, a prayer to the God of my life.

May the LORD: TEV takes this as a prayer, but others see it as a statement, as RSV does.

show his constant love: literally "commands his constant love (to come)" (see RSV).

	TEV	RSV
42.9	To God, my defender, I say, "Why have you forgotten me? Why must I go on suffering from the cruelty of my enemies?"	I say to God, my rock: "Why hast thou forgotten me? Why go I mourning because of the oppression of the enemy?"

my defender: literally "my rock," but with the figurative sense that God defends me in life just as a rock protects me in battle.

	TEV	RSV
42.10	I am crushed by their insults, as they keep on asking me, "Where is your God?"	As with a deadly wound in my body, my adversaries taunt me, while they say to me continually, "Where is your God?"

I am crushed: the Hebrew is unclear, perhaps "with crushing of my bones" or "with a murder of my bones." RSV translates "with a deadly wound in my body," taking "bones" to mean "body." But whatever the specific meaning, the injury is understood figuratively as caused by insults of enemies. Perhaps the meaning is that the psalmist senses the presence of death in his body because of the insults of enemies.

insults: the Hebrew verb means "taunt" (RSV), "reproach," "revile," "say evil things to."

	TEV	RSV
42.11	Why am I so sad? Why am I so troubled? I will put my hope in God, and once again I will praise him, my savior and my God.	Why are you cast down, O my soul, and why are you disquieted within me? Hope in God; for I shall again praise him, my help and my God.

See verse 5.

43.1	TEV	RSV

<table>
<tr><td>O God, declare me innocent,
and defend my cause against
the ungodly;
deliver me from lying and
evil men!</td><td>Vindicate me, O God, and
defend my cause
against an ungodly people;
from deceitful and unjust
men
deliver me!</td></tr>
</table>

declare me innocent: literally "judge me," but here in the sense "pronounce the judgment that will set me free." RSV translates this with "vindicate me."

defend my cause: the Hebrew has in mind the activity of a lawyer, who defends a person before a judge. The psalmist is being attacked in court by ungodly, lying men.

deliver me: "save me," from the attack of evil men.

43.2	TEV	RSV

<table>
<tr><td>You are my protector;
why have you abandoned me?
Why must I go on suffering
from the cruelty of my
enemies?</td><td>For thou art the God in whom
I take refuge;
why hast thou cast me off?
Why go I mourning
because of the oppression
of the enemy?</td></tr>
</table>

my protector: literally "God of my fortress," that is, "God who is like a fortress that protects me." RSV "the God in whom I take refuge." abandoned: "reject, push away," "cast...off" (RSV). See 42.9.

go on suffering: the Hebrew "go dressed in mourning clothes" (RSV "go mourning") is a figure for experiencing suffering and sorrow.

cruelty: "oppression" (RSV), "torment."

43.3	TEV	RSV

<table>
<tr><td>Send your light and your
truth;
may they lead me
and bring me back to Zion,
your sacred hill,^r
and to your Temple, where
you live.</td><td>Oh send out thy light and
thy truth;
let them lead me,
let them bring me to thy
holy hill
and to thy dwelling!</td></tr>
</table>

^rSACRED HILL: *See 2.6.*

light...truth: these are viewed as if they were persons able to lead the psalmist back to the Temple in Jerusalem. In some languages this personification will have to be dropped. Perhaps one might say "...they will help me to return..."

Zion, your sacred hill: the hill in Jerusalem on which the Temple stood. TEV has added Zion to make the identification of "holy hill" (RSV) clear.

	TEV	RSV
43.4

<table>
<tr><td>

TEV

Then I will go to your altar,
    O God;
  you are the source of my
     happiness.
I will play my harp and sing
    praise to you,
  O God, my God.

</td><td>

RSV

Then I will go to the altar
    of God,
  to God my exceeding joy;
  and I will praise thee with
    the lyre,
  O God, my God,

</td></tr>
</table>

<u>your altar, O God</u>: literally "the altar of God" (RSV), but the psalmist has been addressing God, and it is much simpler in English to retain the second person.

<u>you are the source of my happiness</u>: literally "the God of (my) happiness" (see RSV), that is, "the God who gives me happiness." See previous comment for "you."

<u>harp</u>: a hand-held, stringed instrument with a sounding box.

43.5

<table>
<tr><td>

TEV

Why am I so sad?
  Why am I so troubled?
I will put my hope in God,
  and once again I will
     praise him,
  my savior and my God.

</td><td>

RSV

Why are you cast down, O
    my soul,
  and why are you disquieted
    within me?
Hope in God; for I shall
    again praise him,
  my help and my God.

</td></tr>
</table>

See 42.5,11.

P S A L M   45

SECTION HEADING

<u>A Royal Wedding Song</u>[v]: "A Song Sung at the Wedding of a King."

<table>
<tr><td>

TEV

[v]HEBREW TITLE: *A poem by the clan of Korah; a love song.*

</td><td>

RSV

To the choirmaster: according to Lilies. A Maskil of the Sons of Korah; a love song.

</td></tr>
</table>

TEV has placed the Hebrew title in the margin. The meaning of the Hebrew word translated "lilies" is not known, but it probably refers to a musical tune or a musical instrument.

45.1

<table>
<tr><td>

TEV

Beautiful words fill my mind,
  as I compose this song for
    the king.

</td><td>

RSV

My heart overflows with a
  goodly theme;

</td></tr>
</table>

Like the pen of a good writer my tongue is ready with a poem.	I address my verses to the king; my tongue is like the pen of a ready scribe.

Beautiful words: the Hebrew "a good word" may have the sense of "a wonderful message," "a beautiful song," "beautiful words," "a goodly theme" (RSV).

fill my mind: literally "my heart is stirred up," but "heart," the seat of thinking and willing, is the equivalent of "mind" in English. The sense is "I am thinking beautiful thoughts."

I compose this song for the king: the Hebrew has "I will say (sing) my works (song, poem) to the king." TEV has expressed the meaning by concentrating on the point of composition, as RSV has done.

the pen of a good writer: the Hebrew refers to a stylus (for use on clay or wax), but the modern equivalent is a pen. The psalmist compares his tongue to a writing instrument.

45.2

TEV	RSV
You are the most handsome of men; you are an eloquent speaker. God has always blessed you.	You are the fairest of the sons of men; grace is poured upon your lips; therefore God has blessed you for ever.

You: that is, the king, "You, O King."

the most handsome of men: this is the meaning of the Hebrew "fairest of the sons of man" (see RSV), although there is some uncertainty about the exact text.

an eloquent speaker: the Hebrew "agreeableness (favor) is poured on your lips" (see RSV) means "you are favored with the ability to speak well," "God has given you the ability to speak the true message."

God has always blessed: the Hebrew has "therefore" (RSV), but this may point backwards; the king's appearance and ability are a gift from God. The word may be translated "because." The word translated "always" may have the meaning "for ever" (RSV).

45.3

TEV	RSV
Buckle on your sword, mighty king; you are glorious and majestic.	Gird your sword upon your thigh, O mighty one, in your glory and majesty!

Buckle on your sword: the Hebrew "buckle your sword on the (your) side" (see RSV) is redundant in English. The king is now pictured as a conquering warrior king.

you are glorious and majestic: literally "your glory and your majesty," which TEV takes independently, rather than connecting with what goes before (RSV) or follows.

45.4 TEV	RSV
Ride on in majesty to victory	In your majesty ride forth victoriously
for the defense of truth and justice!*w*	for the cause of truth and to defend*g* the right;
Your strength will win you great victories!	let your right hand teach you dread deeds!

w Probable text and justice; Hebrew and meekness of justice.

g Cn: Heb *and the meekness of*

Ride on: this is the picture of a warrior leading his troops, but it should not be understood that he is to go to war on his wedding day, but that he would always be victorious.

in majesty to victory: literally "and (in) your glory (the same word as in verse 3) be successful," but there is considerable uncertainty about the Hebrew text.

for the defense of truth and justice: literally "on a matter of truth and humility (of) justice," but TEV has dropped the Hebrew word for "humility," as the note shows. The Hebrew text is certainly difficult, but it may possibly have the sense of "for the defense of truth, meekness (poverty), and justice" or "for the defense of truth and mild justice."

Your strength: "your right hand" (RSV) is a symbol of strength.

will win you: the Hebrew has "will teach you" or "may it teach you," but "to teach great victories" must have the sense of "perform in such a way as to gain great victories," "perform mighty deeds for you."

great victories: the Hebrew word means "wonderful and fearful things" and seems to refer to battle scenes. RSV translates as "dread deeds."

45.5 TEV	RSV
Your arrows are sharp,	Your arrows are sharp
they pierce the hearts of your enemies;	in the heart of the king's enemies;
nations fall down at your feet.	the peoples fall under you.

they pierce the hearts of your enemies: the Hebrew text has been rearranged in RSV and TEV to provide this interpretation, but the text itself is very uncertain, as the various translations show. Here literally "in the heart of the enemies of the king" at the end of the verse is connected with the first words about sharp arrows.

nations fall down at your feet: literally "peoples fall beneath you," which may mean this, but there is some uncertainty about the text.

45.6 TEV	RSV
The kingdom that God has given you*x*	Your divine throne*h* endures for ever and ever.

will last forever and ever.   Your royal scepter is a
You rule over your people with   scepter of equity;
    justice;

*h*Or *Your throne is a throne of God,*
*x*The kingdom that God has given   or *Thy throne, O God*
you; *or* Your kingdom, O God;
or Your divine kingdom.

The kingdom that God has given you: as the RSV and TEV notes show, the meaning is not clear. The Hebrew, translated literally "your throne God for ever and ever," is interpreted in various ways. It is clear that "throne" is a symbol for the act of reigning, the kingdom, and not just a piece of furniture. TEV interprets "your throne (is) from God (and) ..." Others: "your throne, O God...;" "your throne, O divine king;" "your divine throne." But if the Hebrew word "God" is addressed to the king, this is the only place it occurs in the Old Testament. It seems more likely that the Hebrew is compressed and means something like TEV has given, or perhaps "your throne (O King) is like God's throne; it stands forever." Poetry frequently leaves the precise relationship between terms undefined, and the translator will often find it necessary to identify the connections and restructure to make the meaning clear.

You rule over the people with justice: the Hebrew has "the scepter of your kingdom is a scepter that is level (fair, right)," but the scepter, like "throne," "crown," is a symbol of the act of reigning as king. In cultures in which a scepter (a ceremonial staff or stick) is not a symbol of royalty, one must drop the image, as TEV has done.

45.7	TEV	RSV
	you love what is right and hate what is evil.	you love righteousness and hate wickedness.
	That is why God, your God, has chosen you	Therefore God, your God, has anointed you
	and has poured out more happiness on you than on any other king.	with the oil of gladness above your fellows;

has chosen you and has poured out...happiness: literally "has anointed you...with the oil of gladness" (RSV), but "anoint," that is, pour olive oil on the head in a symbolic way, is the act which designates the king as chosen by God, and for most readers the fact that he is chosen by God is more important than the external act. The TEV translation poured out happiness retains a part of the figure: God gives you happiness as if he had poured olive oil on your head. If the figure cannot be readily retained, one may translate "has chosen you and made you very happy."

more...than on any other king: the Hebrew "more than your fellows" (see RSV) could mean "more than any other man," but probably refers to other kings.

45.8	TEV	RSV
	The perfume of myrrh and aloes is on your clothes; musicians entertain you in palaces decorated with ivory.	your robes are all fragrant with myrrh and aloes and cassia. From ivory palaces stringed instruments make you glad;

The perfume of myrrh and aloes: TEV has identified these products as perfume to help the reader. Myrrh is a sweet-smelling sap or gum from a tree; aloes is a sweet-smelling wood. The Hebrew also has "cassia" (RSV), a sweet-smelling flower or wood.

musicians entertain you: the Hebrew possibly means "stringed instruments make you glad" (RSV), but obviously it is musicians who play the instruments.

palaces decorated with ivory: the Hebrew has "palaces of tooth (elephant's tooth)," but this does not mean "made out of" (RSV "ivory palaces") but "decorated with."

45.9	TEV	RSV
	Among the ladies of your court are daughters of kings, and at the right of your throne stands the queen, wearing ornaments of finest gold.	daughters of kings are among your ladies of honor; at your right hand stands the queen in gold of Ophir.

ladies of your court: the Hebrew "your precious things," usually applied to jewels and the like, is assumed to refer here to the women of the king's harem. The Hebrew text is uncertain.

daughters of kings: some translations change the text to singular.

at the right of your throne: literally "at your right," the place of honor.

wearing ornaments of finest gold: the Hebrew is "in gold of Ophir," but this cannot mean "clothed in gold" or the like and must refer to articles of jewelry. Ophir was famous as the source of fine gold, and the reader needs to know that "gold of Ophir" is fine gold, rather than gold that comes from Ophir.

45.10	TEV	RSV
	Bride of the king, listen to what I say— forget your people and your relatives.	Hear, O daughter, consider, and incline your ear; forget your people and your father's house;

Bride of the king: the Hebrew has "daughter" (RSV), a term of endearment, but it is clear that the words are addressed to the bride.

listen to what I say: this is what is meant by the literal "hear... and see and bend down your ear" (see RSV).

forget: this may indicate that the bride was a foreigner, but in any case she is now asked to give her complete loyalty to her husband and his people.

your relatives: literally "the house of your father," but the term is used to refer to the extended family, the relatives.

45.11	TEV	RSV
	Your beauty will make the king desire you; he is your master, so you must obey him.	and the king will desire your beauty. Since he is your lord, bow to him;

Your beauty will make the king desire you: this gives the sense of the literal "the king will desire your beauty" (RSV).

obey him: the Hebrew "bow down to him" (see RSV) is used to indicate obedience.

45.12	TEV	RSV
	The people of Tyre will bring you gifts; rich people will try to win your favor.	the people^i of Tyre will sue your favor with gifts, the richest of the people

^{i}Heb daughter

The people of Tyre: literally "and the daughter of Tyre," which may refer to the people, but which many take to mean that the king's bride is a woman from Tyre.

will bring you gifts: literally "with gifts." Note that there is considerable uncertainty about the text of these verses, and translations differ greatly as to how these words are connected with each other.

will try to win your favor: this is the meaning of the Hebrew, which RSV translates "sue your favor."

45.13	TEV	RSV
	The princess is in the palace—how beautiful she is! Her gown is made of gold thread.	with all kinds of wealth. The princess is decked in her chamber with gold-woven robes;^{j}

^{j}Or people. All glorious is the princess within, gold embroidery is her clothing

is in the palace...beautiful: this translates "all her wealth (or, splendor)," which some connect with verse 12 (RSV "with all kinds of wealth"), but which TEV has taken in the sense "in all her beauty," and "within" (in the palace), which RSV translates "in her chamber."

45.13

is made of gold thread: that is, gold threads are woven in with other threads to produce the expensive cloth, of which her dress is made.

45.14	TEV	RSV
	In her colorful gown she is led to the king, followed by her bridesmaids, and they also are brought to him.	in many-colored robes she is led to the king, with her virgin companions, her escort,^k in her train.

^kHeb *those brought to you*

followed by her bridesmaids: literally "virgins after her, her companions" that is, her young women friends (bridesmaids) follow her.
they: that is, the bridesmaids, but some understand the reference to be to another group of servants.
to him: the Hebrew text has "to you," but this must mean "to the king" (see verses 2-9), and some Hebrew manuscripts have "to him." RSV takes "brought to him" to mean "her escort."

45.15	TEV	RSV
	With joy and gladness they come and enter the king's palace.	With joy and gladness they are led along as they enter the palace of the king.

they come and enter: literally "they are brought (led)...they enter" (see RSV), which refers to the whole bridal party as it is brought into the palace.

45.16	TEV	RSV
	You, my king, will have many sons to succeed your ancestors as kings, and you will make them rulers over the whole earth.	Instead of your fathers shall be your sons; you will make them princes in all the earth.

You, my king: the words my king are introduced by TEV to help the reader understand that the king is now being addressed, as in verses 2-9.
will have many sons...kings: the Hebrew has "instead of your fathers (ancestors) shall be your sons" (RSV), but this is to be understood as a wish or prayer that as he has succeeded his father, his sons will succeed him as kings; the psalmist prays that the king's line will continue.

45.17	TEV	RSV

<table>
<tr><td>My song will keep your fame
alive forever,
and everyone will praise you
for all time to come.</td><td>I will cause your name to
be celebrated in all
generations;
therefore the peoples will
praise you for ever and
ever.</td></tr>
</table>

<u>My song will keep your fame alive</u>: literally "I will cause your name to be remembered" (see RSV), but the psalmist is thinking of the song he has composed (see verse 1), and it is common in Hebrew for "name" to refer to "fame."

P S A L M   46

SECTION HEADING

<u>God Is with Us</u>ᵞ: "God Will Help Us," "God Will Keep Us Safe."

	TEV	RSV

ᵞHEBREW TITLE: *A song by the clan of Korah.*

To the choirmaster. A Psalm of the Sons of Korah. According to Alamoth. A Song.

TEV has placed the Hebrew title in the margin. "Alamoth" (RSV) seems to be a musical notation, but the meaning is not known. The psalm is divided into three sections (1-3; 4-6; 8-10), each followed by a refrain (now missing from the first).

46.1	TEV	RSV

<table>
<tr><td>God is our shelter and
strength,
always ready to help in
times of trouble.</td><td>God is our refuge and
strength,
a very present^l help in
trouble.</td></tr>
</table>

ˡOr *well proved*

    <u>shelter</u>: "a place of refuge," "a place where one can be protected," but used figuratively to mean "God protects us."
    <u>strength</u>: the meaning is "God gives us strength," "God makes us strong."
    <u>always ready to help</u>: the Hebrew has "a help...easily found," that is "readily accessible." It seems better to state the idea actively. The RSV "a very present help" translates this meaning, but the RSV note translates the words in the sense "found secure."

	TEV	RSV
46.2	So we will not be afraid, even if the earth is shaken and mountains fall into the ocean depths;	Therefore we will not fear though the earth should change, though the mountains shake in the heart of the sea;

So: "because that is true," "therefore" (RSV).

is shaken: the Hebrew verb probably has the meaning "quake," "shake," as in an earthquake, but others take it to mean "be changed" (see RSV).

fall into: the Hebrew verb means "stagger," "stumble," and may have the sense "fall," but the meaning may be that the foundation of the mountains (reaching to the ocean depths) shake and break up.

ocean depths: this is the sense of the literal "heart of the sea" (RSV), the deep part of the sea.

	TEV	RSV
46.3	even if the seas roar and rage, and the hills are shaken by the violence.	though its waters roar and foam, though the mountains tremble with its tumult. *Selah*

seas: literally "its waters" (RSV), but this refers to the seas.

roar and rage: literally "make a loud noise (as the waves of the sea) and foam," which is a way of picturing a storm on the seas.

hills: or "mountains," the same word as in verse 2.

are shaken: the Hebrew word is not the same as in verse 2, but the idea is the same.

violence: the word probably refers to high, violent waves (so RSV "tumult"), but some take it as referring to the idea that God is high above the world.

	TEV	RSV
46.4	There is a river that brings joy to the city of God, to the sacred house of the Most High.	There is a river whose streams make glad the city of God, the holy habitation of the Most High.

river: there is no river in Jerusalem. The psalmist is using "river" in a figurative way and is probably thinking of the river in the Garden of Eden (Gen 2.10). The Hebrew has "a river, its channel" (RSV "a river whose streams"), which could refer to one stream of a larger river, but this is not likely.

the city of God: that is, Jerusalem.

the sacred house of the Most High: this seems to be the meaning of the Hebrew text and is a reference to the Temple as the dwelling place of God.

46.5 TEV	RSV
God is in that city, and it will never be destroyed; at early dawn he will come to its aid.	God is in the midst of her, she shall not be moved; God will help her right early.

be destroyed: literally "be shaken" (see verse 2), but the sense of "shaken so hard that it falls into ruins," "be overthrown." This is also intended by RSV "be moved." One might translate "no army or enemy will ever destroy that city."

at early dawn: the early morning was traditionally considered a time for God's answer and help, perhaps out of the idea that the night is darkest just before the dawn or that the attack of enemies often comes at dawn. TEV translates more directly than RSV, "right early."

46.6 TEV	RSV
Nations are terrified, kingdoms are shaken; God thunders, and the earth dissolves.	The nations rage, the kingdoms totter; he utters his voice, the earth melts.

are terrified: the same Hebrew verb is translated "roar" in verse 3; here "make a loud noise" is seen as the result of fear, that is, they are in tumult because of fear. RSV "rage" would place the emphasis on making loud noise in anger. It is possible that the sense is that of political turmoil and disturbance, parallel to kingdoms are shaken, that is, "are overthrown, destroyed."

thunders: the Hebrew "gives (with) his voice" (see RSV) is a way of speaking of thunder, as is generally agreed.

dissolves: "melts" (RSV), probably to be understood figuratively, in fear and terror.

46.7 TEV	RSV
The LORD Almighty is with us; the God of Jacob is our refuge.	The LORD of hosts is with us; the God of Jacob is our refuge.^{m} Selah

^{m}Or *fortress*

The LORD Almighty: literally "the LORD of armies" (RSV "the LORD of hosts"), who leads his armies into battle and is victorious over his enemies.

is with us: "will protect us," "will take care of us."

the God of Jacob: that is, "the God whom Jacob worshiped," or perhaps "the God who leads the people of Israel."

our refuge: "a place of safety" (see verse 1). The meaning is "he will keep us safe, will protect us."

46.8 TEV	RSV

Come and see what the
   LORD has done.
See what amazing things
   he has done on earth.
	Come, behold the works of
	   the LORD,
	how he has wrought desolations
	   in the earth.

Come and see: this is not a literal invitation to go somewhere and look but a figurative use: "consider," "pay attention to this fact."

amazing things: the Hebrew word means "something that causes one to be afraid and marvel," here possibly of the destructive power of the LORD in punishing enemies.

46.9 TEV	RSV

He stops wars all over the
   world;
he breaks bows, destroys
   spears,
and sets shields on fire.
	He makes wars cease to the
	   end of the earth;
	he breaks the bow, and
	   shatters the spear,
	he burns the chariots
	   with fire!

He stops wars: "brings wars to an end," "puts an end to wars." The breaking of weapons indicates that the instruments of war are no longer useful.

shields: it is now generally agreed that the Hebrew word refers to shields and not to war wagons (RSV "chariots").

46.10 TEV	RSV

"Stop fighting," he says,
   "and know that I am
   God,
supreme among the nations,
supreme over the world."
	"Be still, and know that
	   I am God.
	I am exalted among the
	   nations,
	I am exalted in the earth!"

Stop fighting: the traditional translation "be still" (RSV) does not express the meaning of the Hebrew "stop," which relates to the ending of fighting.

he says: these words are introduced in TEV to help the reader recognize that the LORD is now speaking to the people.

know: "acknowledge," "confess."

supreme: the Hebrew has "I am high," but with the figurative meaning "I am the king, the ruler, over the nations and the world."

46.11 TEV	RSV

The LORD Almighty is with us;
   the God of Jacob is our
     refuge.
	The LORD of hosts is with us;
	   the God of Jacob is our
	     refuge.^m Selah

^mOr fortress

See verse 7.

PSALM 51

SECTION HEADING

A Prayer for Forgiveness[j]: "Confession and Forgiveness," "A Prayer for Forgiveness and Renewal."

TEV	RSV
[j]HEBREW TITLE: *A psalm by David, after the prophet Nathan had spoken to him about his adultery with Bathsheba.*	To the choirmaster. A Psalm of David, when Nathan the prophet came to him, after he had gone in to Bathsheba.

TEV has placed the Hebrew title in the margin. Most scholars do not believe that the Hebrew title reflects the actual circumstances in which the psalm was written; the Hebrew title was added at some time after the psalm was written, but shows how a later generation understood the psalm.

51.1-2 TEV	RSV
Be merciful to me, O God, because of your constant love. Because of your great mercy wipe away my sins! 2 Wash away all my evil and make me clean from my sin!	Have mercy on me, O God, according to thy stead- fast love; according to thy abundant mercy blot out my trans- gressions. 2 Wash me thoroughly from my iniquity, and cleanse me from my sin!

Be merciful: "show kindness," "be gracious."
wipe away: in Hebrew the verbs "wipe away," "wash away," and "make clean" are used figuratively: just as a dirty mark can be wiped off (or dirty clothes washed or a dirty floor scrubbed), so sin can be removed from a person. In some languages this comparison may have to be stated specifically.
sins...evil: three Hebrew words are used in these verses with no sharp distinction in meaning. The translator need not try to manufacture three different words for "transgression," "iniquity," "sin."

51.3 TEV	RSV
I recognize my faults; I am always conscious of my sins.	For I know my transgressions, and my sin is ever before me.

faults: the same Hebrew word is translated "sins" in verse 1.
recognize: literally "know" (RSV), but with the sense "acknowl-edge," "confess," "admit."

[69]

51.3

I am...conscious: the Hebrew "is before me" (RSV) means " I am aware," "I can see."

51.4

TEV	RSV

I have sinned against you—
   only against you—
and done what you consider
   evil.
So you are right in judging
   me;
   you are justified in con-
   demning me.
	Against thee, thee only, have
	   I sinned,
	and done that which is evil
	   in thy sight,
	so that thou art justified in
	   thy sentence
	and blameless in thy
	   judgment.

only against you: the psalmist confesses that his sin (whatever it was) was against God.

what you consider evil: this correctly translates "what is evil in your eyes."

in judging me: literally "in your word," that is, "in the sentence (RSV) of judgment that you give."

you are justified: literally "you are pure (blameless)" (RSV), that is, "you do nothing wrong," "what you do is right."

51.5

TEV	RSV

I have been evil from the
   day I was born;
   from the time I was con-
   cieved, I have been
   sinful.
	Behold, I was brought forth
	   in iniquity,
	and in sin did my mother
	   conceive me.

evil from the day I was born: literally "in sin I was born" (see RSV), but the psalmist is only thinking of the fact that he is a sinner through and through.

from the time I was conceived, I have been sinful: literally "in sin my mother conceived me," but the psalmist is not speaking of the sexual act as transmitting sin or anything like that; he is using figurative language to say that his whole being, from beginning to end, is sinful. A literal translation might be interpreted to mean that the mother conceived the child in adultery.

51.6

TEV	RSV

Sincerity and truth are
   what you require;
   fill my mind with your
   wisdom.
	Behold, thou desirest truth
	   in the inward being;
	   therefore teach me wisdom
	   in my secret heart.

Sincerity and truth are what you require: the Hebrew is difficult, perhaps "you take pleasure in truth in secret (within)" (see RSV), but the meaning is not at all certain. The translator should probably simply follow one of the translations at this point.

my mind: the Hebrew is difficult, perhaps "in what is secret" (which possibly could mean the heart), but the meaning is uncertain. RSV "my secret heart" seems to mean a second heart, but this is not intended by the Hebrew.

51.7	TEV	RSV
	Remove my sin, and I will be clean; wash me, and I will be whiter than snow.	Purge me with hyssop, and I shall be clean; wash me, and I shall be whiter than snow.

Remove my sin: a literal translation of the Hebrew would give something like "de-sin me with hyssop" (see RSV). Hyssop was a small bushy plant used in ceremonies of atonement and purification to sprinkle water and blood on people and things. TEV has chosen to abandon the literal language and to give the meaning, since the psalmist is really praying for inner forgiveness, not external purification.

wash me: this is the same as one of the verbs in verse 2.

whiter than snow: snow was rare in Palestine, but it served as a proverbial comparison for whiteness. Where it is not known, some other natural comparison may be used.

51.8	TEV	RSV
	Let me hear the sounds of joy and gladness; and though you have crushed me and broken me, I will be happy once again.	Fill^x me with joy and gladness; let the bones which thou hast broken rejoice.

^{x}Syr: Heb *Make to hear*

Let me hear: literally "you will cause me to hear," which possibly means "forgive me so that I can hear." There is little reason to change the text and follow RSV "fill."

and though you have crushed me...I will be happy once again: literally "bones which you broke shall shout with joy" (see RSV). TEV understands this to refer to emotional distress rather than physical illness, which is caused by the Lord. When he restores the psalmist, there will be rejoicing.

51.9	TEV	RSV
	Close your eyes to my sins and wipe out all my evil.	Hide thy face from my sins, and blot out all my iniquities.

Close your eyes: the Hebrew has "hide your face," but the sense is "do not look upon my sins," meaning "forgive my sins."

wipe out: the same Hebrew verb is translated "wipe away" in verse 1. RSV used "blot out" in both verses.

	TEV		RSV

<table>
<tr><td>51.10</td><td>TEV</td><td>RSV</td></tr>
</table>

51.10   TEV

Create a pure heart in me,
   O God,
  and put a new and loyal
    spirit in me.

RSV

Create in me a clean heart,
   O God,
  and put a new and right^{y}
    spirit within me.

^{y}Or *steadfast*

Create: the Hebrew verb is the same one used for the activity of
God in creating the world.
    a pure heart: RSV "clean heart," but remember that "heart" means
"mind," "will," and the meaning will be "single-mindedness, " thus
"Let me think of you, O God."
    a new and loyal spirit: RSV "a new and right spirit," but the
Hebrew word for "spirit" has the meaning of "will," "mind," "attitude,"
and not "spirit" as opposed to "body." Here the idea is "make me obedient."

51.11   TEV

Do not banish me from your
   presence;
  do not take your holy spirit
   away from me.

RSV

Cast me not away from thy
   presence,
  and take not thy holy
   Spirit from me.

banish: literally "throw away," that is, "dismiss," "remove."
    your holy spirit: the words do not have the developed sense that
is found in the New Testament. Here the Hebrew words "the spirit of
your holiness" have the same meaning as "your presence" in the first
line of the verse. God's "breath/wind/spirit" (and the Hebrew word can
have all of these meanings) is the power of the Lord, creating, sustain-
ing, and making life possible. If your holy spirit is likely to be
misunderstood in the sense of "your Holy Spirit" in the New Testament,
it will be better to use "your spirit."

51.12   TEV

Give me again the joy that
   comes from your salvation,
  and make me willing to obey
   you.

RSV

Restore to me the joy of
   thy salvation,
  and uphold me with a willing spirit.

the joy that comes from your salvation: that is, "the joy I have
when I know that you have saved me." One might translate "make me happy
again through your help" or "help me, and make me happy again."
    make me willing to obey you: the Hebrew has "support me (or provide
me) with a willing spirit," in which "willing spirit" is a description
of the obedient attitude that the psalmist asks from God. See verse 10.

51.13   TEV

Then I will teach sinners
   your commands,

RSV

Then I will teach trans-
   gressors thy ways,

| and they will turn back to
  you. | and sinners will return to
  thee. |

Then I will teach: RSV and TEV take the Hebrew to be a promise that if God forgives the psalmist's sin, he will teach sinners what God wants them to know.

your commands: the Hebrew "your ways" (RSV) means "the rules God gives to his people for living their lives."

51.14 TEV	RSV

Spare my life, O God, and
    save me,^{k}
and I will gladly proclaim
    your righteousness.
	Deliver me from blood-
	    guiltiness,^{z} O God,
	thou God of my Salvation,
	and my tongue will sing
	    aloud of thy deliverance.

^{k}Spare my life...me; *or* O God my
savior, keep me from the crime
of murder.

^{z}Or *death*

Spare my life...and save me: literally "rescue me from blood(s)... God of my salvation"; as the TEV margin shows, it is not clear whether "blood" refers to the death of the psalmist or to an act of murder that he might commit, but the former is more likely. RSV has assumed that murder is more likely and has placed "death" in the margin.

and I will gladly proclaim: the Hebrew "my tongue will proclaim with shouts of joy" has the sense "if you save me, I will tell with joy..."

51.15 TEV	RSV

Help me to speak, Lord,
    and I will praise you.
	O Lord, open thou my lips,
	    and my mouth shall show
	      forth thy praise.

Help me to speak: literally "open my lips" (RSV), but the request is not to have an open mouth; it is to speak.

I: the Hebrew has "my mouth" (RSV), but this is a way of speaking of the activity of the person.

51.16 TEV	RSV

You do not want sacrifices,
    or I would offer them;
you are not pleased with
    burnt offerings.
	For thou hast no delight in
	    sacrifice;
	were I to give a burnt
	    offering, thou wouldst
	    not be pleased.

or I would offer them: TEV has connected this statement with the preceding statement, as the standard Hebrew text does, but most translations connect with the following, as RSV does.

51.17 TEV	RSV
My sacrifice is a humble spirit, O God; you will not reject a humble and repentant heart.	The sacrifice acceptable to God[a] is a broken spirit; a broken and contrite heart, O God, thou wilt not despise.

[a]Or *My sacrifice, O God*

My sacrifice...O God: the standard Hebrew text has "the sacrifices of God," which is often interpreted "the sacrifice that God desires." TEV (along with other translations) has made a slight change in the Hebrew vowels. RSV has translated the standard text and placed the other possibility in the margin.

a humble spirit: the Hebrew "a broken spirit" is to be understood in the sense of a "determination to obey God." One speaks, for example, of breaking a horse when one compels it to obey its rider.

a humble and repentant heart: literally "a broken and crushed heart," but "heart" is the seat of willing, thinking. The psalmist is stating his faith that God will accept him when he repents and obeys.

51.18 TEV	RSV
O God, be kind to Zion and help her; rebuild the walls of Jerusalem.	Do good to Zion in thy good pleasure; rebuild the walls of Jerusalem,

be kind to: "do good to" (RSV), "cause things to go well for." The last two verses are generally recognized as a later addition to the original psalm, reflecting a time when Jerusalem was in ruins.

help her: the Hebrew "in your favor" (RSV "in thy good pleasure") refers to God's blessings.

51.19 TEV	RSV
Then you will be pleased with proper sacrifices and with our burnt offerings; and bulls will be sacrificed on your altar.	then wilt thou delight in right sacrifices, in burnt offerings and whole burnt offerings; then bulls will be offered on thy altar.

proper: RSV "right," that is, the sacrifices that were required by the Law of Moses.

burnt offerings: literally "burnt offerings and whole burnt offerings" (RSV). Some translations and scholars omit this as a later addition to the text.

PSALM 63

SECTION HEADING

Longing for God[d]: "(To Have) God's Love is Better Than Life."

TEV	RSV
[d]HEBREW TITLE: *A psalm by David,*	A Psalm of David, when he was in
when he was in the desert of	the Wilderness of Judah.
Judea.	

TEV has placed the Hebrew title in a note.

63.1

TEV	RSV

O God, you are my God,
    and I long for you.
My whole being desires you;
    like a dry, worn-out, and
        waterless land,
my soul is thirsty for you.
	O God, thou art my God, I
	    seek thee,
	    my soul thirsts for thee;
	    my flesh faints for thee,
	    as in a dry and weary land
	        where no water is.

I long for you: the Hebrew verb has the sense "be intent on," "long for," "seek" (RSV). Some scholars assume that it also has reference to the dawn, "seek early."

My whole being...my soul: literally "my soul...my flesh" (RSV), but in Hebrew thought this includes the whole of man: the life principle (breath from God) and the material.

desires you: the psalmist's desire for God is expressed in terms of thirst. He has a desire for God like a man's thirst for water or like a dry, parched land in need of rain.

like: the standard Hebrew text has "in," but some Hebrew manuscripts have "like," which suits the context better.

worn-out: "exhausted," "of no value."

63.2

TEV	RSV

Let me see you in the
    sanctuary;
    let me see how mighty and
        glorious you are.
	So I have looked upon thee
	    in the sanctuary,
	    beholding thy power and
	        glory.

Let me see you: TEV has understood the Hebrew verb as a wish, which seems more likely than a statement about past or future. RSV has understood it as a past event.

sanctuary: literally "the holy place," that is, the Temple.

63.3

TEV	RSV

Your constant love is better
    than life itself,
	Because thy steadfast love
	    is better than life,

and so I will praise you.   my lips will praise thee.

constant love: the Hebrew word expresses the ideas of "love," "loyalty," "faithfulness."
I: the Hebrew has "my lips" (RSV), but the psalmist praises God by speaking with his mouth and lips.

63.4	TEV	RSV
	I will give you thanks as long as I live; I will raise my hands to you in prayer.	So I will bless thee as long as I live; I will lift up my hands and call on thy name.

give you thanks: the Hebrew word "bless" has the sense of "give praise and thanks" when it is used about God.
raise my hands to you in prayer: literally "in your name I will lift up my hands," but standing with raised arms is a posture of prayer, and "in your name" refers to calling upon the Lord in prayer.

63.5	TEV	RSV
	My soul will feast and be satisfied, and I will sing glad songs of praise to you.	My soul is feasted as with marrow and fat, and my mouth praises thee with joyful lips,

will feast and be satisfied: the Hebrew expresses this with "be satisfied as with fat and marrow," but the psalmist is comparing his spiritual experience with a great feast, and fat is considered to be the best part of the meat, the best food. But it seems better to abandon the figure and use "feast." Note that TEV connects verse 5 with verse 4, while RSV connects it with verse 6. The connection with what precedes seems to make better sense.
I will sing glad songs of praise: the Hebrew has "my mouth praises with joyful lips" (RSV), but lips are joyful only in the sense that joyful songs are being sung.

63.6	TEV	RSV
	As I lie in bed, I remember you; all night long I think of you,	when I think of thee upon my bed, and meditate on thee in the watches of the night;

all night long: literally "in the night watches" (see RSV), but this means in each of the night watches (three or four hours each), that is, throughout the night.

63.7	TEV	RSV
	because you have always been my help.	for thou hast been my help,

In the shadow of your wings
    I sing for joy.
	and in the shadow of thy
	    wings I sing for joy.

have always been my help: that is, "because you have always helped me."

shadow of your wings: the psalmist feels safe because he is in the Temple and pictures himself under the wings of the winged creatures that overshadowed the Covenant Box. It is also possible but less likely that the psalmist pictures God as a mother hen protecting her chicks.

63.8 TEV	RSV

I cling to you,
  and your hand keeps me
    safe.
	My soul clings to thee;
	  thy right hand upholds me.

I cling to you: literally "my soul (my being, I) clings close to you" (see RSV), that is, the psalmist expresses in terms of space his longing to be near God.

your hand: this is a way of speaking of God's power. The Hebrew text has "right hand" (RSV).

keep me safe: literally "holds me (firmly)" (see RSV), in such a way that I am protected.

63.9 TEV	RSV

Those who are trying to
    kill me
  will go down into the
    world of the dead.
	But those who seek to
	    destroy my life
	  shall go down into the
	    depths of the earth;

are trying to kill me: the Hebrew speaks clearly of "those who seek my life," that is, try to kill me, but there is an additional Hebrew word, the meaning of which is not certain, perhaps "to destruction" or "without cause" or "for evil."

the world of the dead: the Hebrew "the lower parts of the earth" reflects the idea that Sheol, the place of the departed dead, was beneath the surface of the earth.

63.10 TEV	RSV

They will be killed in
    battle,
  and their bodies eaten
    by wolves.
	they shall be given over
	    to the power of the
	    sword,
	  they shall be prey for
	    jackals.

be killed in battle: the Hebrew is not clear but probably means "shall be given over to the hands of the sword" (see RSV), that is, "shall be killed with the sword (in battle)," "shall die in war."

their bodies eaten by wolves: this translates "they shall be a portion for (given to) jackals/wolves (a dog-like animal)," but the sense is that their bodies will be left in the fields for these wild animals to eat.

63.11	TEV	RSV

	Because God gives him
	    victory,
	  the king will rejoice.
	Those who make promises
	    in God's name will
	    praise him,
	  but the mouths of liars
	    will be shut.
		But the king shall rejoice
		    in God;
		  all who swear by him shall
		    glory;
		  for the mouths of liars will
		    be stopped.

Because God gives him victory: the Hebrew has only "in God," that is, because of what God has done for him. The sudden reference to the king may be an expression of the idea that the Temple is under the protection of the king.

the king will rejoice: in many languages it may be necessary to restore the Hebrew order (as in RSV) or else read in the first line "Because God gives the king victory." It may also be helpful to introduce a contrast, "But God will give the king victory, and he will rejoice" or "But the king will rejoice because God gives him the victory."

Those who make promises in God's name: literally "those who take oaths by him" (RSV "who swear by him"), that is, those who use the name of the Lord in making their vows; for example, "I promise in the name of the Lord that I will do so and so." It is possible, but less likely, that the sense is "make promises in the name of the king."

will be shut: stopped (RSV), so that they will no longer be able to speak.

P S A L M   67

SECTION HEADING

A Song of Thanksgiving[k]: "Thanksgiving at Harvest," "All People Will Praise God."

	TEV	RSV
[k]HEBREW TITLE:	*A psalm; a song.*	To the choirmaster: with stringed instruments. A Psalm. A Song.

TEV has placed the Hebrew title in the footnote.

67.1	TEV	RSV

	God, be merciful to us and
	  bless us;
		May God be gracious to us
		  and bless us

[78]

```
    look on us with kindness,           and make his face to shine
                                          upon us,        Selah
```

look on us with kindness: the Hebrew "make his face to shine on us" (RSV) is a figurative way of speaking of God's kindness and mercy. See the priestly prayer in Numbers 6.24-26. The Hebrew word "Selah" here and at the end of verse 4 need not be translated. See the discussion at 24.6.

67.2

TEV	RSV
so that the whole world may know your will;	that thy way may be known upon earth,
so that all nations may know your salvation.	thy saving power among all nations.

your will: the Hebrew has "your way" (some manuscripts have "your ways"), but this means "the paths (the kind of life) you want your people to follow (live)," that is, "what you want your people to do."
your salvation: the Hebrew word means "help," "prosperity," "salvation." One might translate "that you have saved (or, always save) your people."

67.3

TEV	RSV
May the peoples praise you, O God;	Let the peoples praise thee, O God;
may all the peoples praise you!	let all the peoples praise thee!

This call for universal praise is repeated as a refrain in verse 5. The verb form is a command.

67.4

TEV	RSV
May the nations be glad and sing for joy,	Let the nations be glad and sing for joy,
because you judge the peoples with justice	for thou dost judge the peoples with equity
and guide every nation on earth.	and guide the nations upon earth. Selah

you judge the peoples with justice: the nations are asked to praise the Lord because he is fair in his ruling over the world and in the decisions he makes.
guide: "lead," "direct." God is ruler of all the nations.

67.5

TEV	RSV
May the peoples praise you, O God;	Let the peoples praise thee, O God;

may all the peoples praise you!	let all the peoples praise thee!

See verse 3.

67.6

TEV	RSV
The land has produced its harvest; God, our God, has blessed us.	The earth has yielded its increase; God, our God, has blessed us.

The land has produced: and this is the basis for the thanksgiving. But some take the verb as a prayer, "may the land produce." If taken in this way, the next line would also be a prayer, "may God bless us."

67.7

TEV	RSV
God has blessed us; may all people everywhere honor him.	God has blessed us; let all the ends of the earth fear him!

all people everywhere: the Hebrew "all the ends of the earth" (RSV) means the people in the farthest parts of the earth, as well as those near at hand.

P S A L M   84

SECTION HEADING

Longing for God's House[w]: "A Pilgrim at the Temple Door," "A Song Sung in Entering the Temple."

TEV	RSV
[w]HEBREW TITLE: *A psalm by the clan of Korah.*	To the choirmaster: according to The Gittith. A Psalm of the Sons of Korah.

TEV has placed the Hebrew title in the footnote.

84.1

TEV	RSV
How I love your Temple, LORD Almighty!	How lovely is thy dwelling place, O LORD of hosts!

How I love your Temple: literally "how beloved (or lovely) are your dwellings," but this is a clear reference to the Temple and the psalmist's love for it, or perhaps his appreciation of its beauty.

    LORD Almighty: the Hebrew "LORD of armies" (RSV "LORD of hosts") means "the LORD who leads the (heavenly) armies," with the ultimate meaning "the LORD of heaven and earth." See 24.10.

84.2	TEV	RSV
	How I want to be there!	My soul longs, yea, faints
	I long to be in the LORD's	for the courts of the LORD;
	Temple.	my heart and flesh sing for
	With my whole being I sing	joy
	for joy	to the living God.
	to the living God.	

    I: the Hebrew has "my soul" (RSV), but this is a way of speaking of the total living person, and not just some part of him.

    the LORD's Temple: that is the meaning of "the courts of the LORD" (RSV), a poetic way of speaking of the Temple. One might translate "the courts of your (the LORD's) Temple."

    With my whole being: here also "my heart and my flesh" (see RSV) refers to the whole person. A parallel English idiom is "with body and soul."

    the living God: he is not only alive, but is the source of life.

84.3	TEV	RSV
	Even the sparrows have	Even the sparrow finds
	built a nest,	a home,
	and the swallows have	and the swallow a nest
	their own home;	for herself,
	they keep their young	where she may lay her
	near your altars,	young,
	LORD Almighty, my king	at thy altars, O LORD of
	and my God.	hosts,
		my King and my God.

    the sparrows...the swallows: the Hebrew (in the singular used in a general way) refers to birds in general and to a particular type of relatively small bird, but it will not be necessary for the translator to identify these birds precisely. Local birds that might nest in and around tall buildings will be satisfactory.

    have built a nest: literally "has found a house," but for birds this will mean a nest, and "find" in Hebrew does not necessarily mean that the birds came upon a nest that had already been built.

    their own home: literally "a nest (room) for themselves."

    altars: the Hebrew plural may have been used for emphasis, or there may be a reference to the altar for sacrifices and the one for incense that were in the Temple.

84.4	TEV	RSV
	How happy are those who	Blessed are those who

```
        live in your Temple,              dwell in thy house,
      always singing praise to          ever singing thy praise!
      you.                                                 Selah
```

How happy: the Hebrew word means "fortunate," "happy," "to be
congratulated," as in 1.1. The traditional translation "blessed" (RSV)
gives the wrong meaning.

those who live in your Temple: this may refer to the officials who
live in the Temple, but it is more likely that the reference is to
those who may worship there at any time. If a pronoun is used ("those
who") the translator should take care that it does not seem to refer
back to sparrows and swallows of verse 3. For "Selah" at the end of
this verse and in verse 8, see 67.1 and 24.6.

84.5   TEV   RSV
```
      How happy are those whose          Blessed are the men whose
        strength comes from                strength is in thee,
        you,                             in whose heart are the
      who are eager to make the            highways to Zion.ʳ
        pilgrimage to Mount Zion.
```
$$^r\text{Heb lacks } to\ Zion$$

whose strength comes from you: the Hebrew has "his (their) strength
is in you" (see RSV) or "his (their) refuge (place of safety) is in
you." The Hebrew word may have either meaning, but in this context it
may be more meaningful to think of those who come to the Temple to seek
safety. If the first is chosen, one may translate "who depend upon you
(for strength)."

who are eager to make the pilgrimage to Mount Zion: the Hebrew has
"the highways (are) in their hearts" (see RSV), which TEV interprets to
mean that they have a deep longing to travel the roads that lead to the
Temple. Some others assume that the Hebrew text should be "praises
are in their hearts." Both RSV and TEV have supplied "Zion," the poetic
name of Jerusalem.

84.6   TEV   RSV
```
      As they pass through the          As they go through the
        dry valley of Baca,               valley of Baca
      it becomes a place of             they make it a place
        springs;                          of springs;
      the autumn rain fills it          the early rain also
        with pools.                       covers it with pools.
```

the dry valley of Baca: the location of the valley of Baca is not
known, but from the context it appears to be a dry valley through which
the pilgrims travel on their way to the Temple. The thought is that the
LORD provides water for the pilgrim travelers even in the most difficult
places.

it becomes a place of springs: literally "they make it a spring
(or, a place of springs)" (see RSV). The thought is that the LORD

blesses them wherever they walk. TEV with it becomes has assumed that
the "they" is used in an impersonal way.

autumn rain: literally "early rain," which in Palestine is the
autumn rain.

pools: the standard Hebrew text has "blessings," but a change of
vowels produces "pools." Several of the words in the Hebrew text are
difficult to interpret, and the translator will probably do best to
follow one of the standard translations.

84.7	TEV	RSV
	They grow stronger as they go;	They go from strength to strength;
	they will see the God of gods on Zion.	the God of gods will be seen in Zion.

They grow stronger as they go: the Hebrew "They go from strength
to strength" (RSV) has the sense that they get stronger with each step.
Others take the Hebrew to mean "from (outer) wall to (inner) wall,"
that is, they move into the city and the Temple.

they will see: literally "he appears," "will be seen" (RSV), which
TEV has made active as better expressing the meaning in English. One
might also consider "they will appear before you, the God of gods, on
Mount Zion."

the God of gods: there is a textual problem, but this seems to be
the correct text. The meaning is that God is greater than all other gods
and rules over them.

84.8	TEV	RSV
	Hear my prayer, LORD God Almighty.	O LORD God of hosts, hear my prayer;
	Listen, O God of Jacob!	give ear, O God of Jacob! _Selah_

Listen: the Hebrew means something like "use the ear," but the
meaning is "listen."

84.9	TEV	RSV
	Bless our king, O God,	Behold our shield, O God;
	the king you have chosen.	look upon the face of thine anointed!

Bless our king: the Hebrew has "see our shield," where "shield"
is to be understood in a figurative way, "our protector." This may
refer to God himself, but it is more likely that the reference is to
the king, and the "see" is to be understood as addressed to God, as
RSV and TEV have taken it. The literal "see...look on the face of" is
then understood as a prayer that God will bless the king.

you have chosen: literally "your anointed" (RSV), but to anoint
(to put olive oil on the head of) has the sense of "choose and set

apart as king." In many cultures the figurative act of putting olive
oil on the head of a person would not be understood, and it is better
to express the meaning without the figure.

84.10 TEV	RSV
One day spent in your Temple is better than a thousand anywhere else; I would rather stand at the gate of the house of my God than live in the homes of the wicked.	For a day in thy courts is better than a thousand elsewhere. I would rather be a door-keeper in the house of my God than dwell in the tents of wickedness.

    your Temple: that is the meaning of "your courts" (RSV). See
verse 2.
    anywhere else: the Hebrew has simply "than a thousand," which is
taken as a natural shortening of "than a thousand days in any other
place." RSV has "elsewhere."
    stand at the gate: the Hebrew has "lie at the threshold," possibly
with the sense "be a beggar," or simply as one waiting to be let in
through the gate, as TEV has taken it. RSV and others interpret the
Hebrew to refer to a "doorkeeper" (possibly an official position), but
this seems less likely.
    homes: the word "tents" (RSV) is often used in Hebrew in the sense
of "dwellings," "homes."

84.11 TEV	RSV
The LORD is our protector and glorious king, blessing us with kindness and honor. He does not refuse any good thing to those who do what is right.	For the LORD God is a sun and shield; he bestows favor and honor. No good thing does the LORD withhold from those who walk uprightly.

    our protector and glorious king: literally "a sun and shield"
(RSV), understood as figures for the king, in this case, the LORD as
king. TEV has taken "shield" as an expression for "our protector" and
"sun" as "our glorious king." Others assume that the Hebrew word "sun"
here refers to a sun-shaped shield, that is, "our great protector."
    do what is right: the Hebrew "walk perfectly" (RSV "walk uprightly")
is a figure for the kind of life that is lived.

84.12 TEV	RSV
LORD Almighty, how happy are those who trust in you!	O LORD of hosts, blessed is the man who trusts in thee!

trust: "have confidence in," "feel safe with."

P S A L M   90

SECTION HEADING

Of God and Man^i: "God is Eternal and Man is Feeble" or "...Temporal" or "...Mortal."

	TEV	RSV
^{i}HEBREW TITLE:	A Prayer by Moses, the man of God.	A Prayer of Moses, the man of God.

TEV has placed the Hebrew title in the footnote.

90.1

TEV	RSV
O Lord, you have always been our home.	Lord, thou hast been our dwelling place^e in all generations.

^{e}Another reading is refuge

always: the Hebrew has "from generation to generation," that is, throughout our whole history.

home: the Hebrew word has the sense of "lair, den," and is often translated as "dwelling place, home," but it is entirely possible that the word here has the meaning of "help," "place of safety." Some Hebrew manuscripts have a different text, which means "place of refuge," reflected in the RSV footnote.

90.2

TEV	RSV
Before you created the hills or brought the world into being, you were eternally God, and will be God forever.	Before the mountains were brought forth, or ever thou hadst formed the earth and the world, from everlasting to everlasting thou art God.

you created: the Hebrew has a passive, "were born" (RSV "were brought forth"); clearly it is the Lord who is the actor, and in many languages the figure of God bringing the mountains to birth will not be understood. In such cases it is better to state the meaning directly, as TEV has done.

the world: the Hebrew has two words (perhaps: the earth and the continents), but it is not necessary to retain two words in translation when one word covers the whole idea. The RSV has "the earth and the world," but the meaning is not clear.

[85]

brought...into being: the Hebrew "brought to birth," "bore" (RSV "formed"), is essentially the same figure as in the first part of the verse.

you were...and will be...forever: the Hebrew "from eternity to eternity" (see RSV) means from the beginning of time to the end of time.

90.3

	TEV	RSV

You tell man to return to
   what he was;
 you change him back to
   dust.

Thou turnest man back to the
   dust,
and sayest, "Turn back, O
   children of men!"

You tell man: TEV changes the order of the elements of the verse and uses indirect discourse instead of direct. Here "man" means "man-kind," "all people." The Hebrew has both "man" and "sons of men," which have a general meaning here. RSV translates the latter as "children of men."

to return to what he was: the Hebrew has "turn" (see RSV), but both parts of the verse refer to death and the fact that the time of a person's death is in the control of God.

90.4

	TEV	RSV

A thousand years to you are
   like one day;
 they are like yesterday,
   already gone,
 like a short hour in the
   night.

For a thousand years in
   thy sight
are but as yesterday when
   it is past,
or as a watch in the
   night.

to you: the Hebrew has "in your eyes," that is, "as you consider things," "as you are concerned," in contrast to the human situation.

a short hour in the night: literally "a night watch," a period of three or four hours, an expression for a short period of time.

90.5

	TEV	RSV

You carry us away like a
   flood;
 we last no longer than a
   dream.
We are like weeds that
   sprout in the morning,

Thou dost sweep men away;
 they are like a dream,
like grass which is re-
   newed in the morning:

You carry us away like a flood: the meaning of the Hebrew is un-certain, and the verb occurs only here. Such things as "put an end to life," "carry away like a flood," "sweep away" (RSV) are proposed as the meaning. Many suggestions have been made for changing the text, but the translator is advised to follow one of the standard translations.

we last no longer than a dream: the meaning of the Hebrew is uncertain, perhaps literally "they shall be asleep," which RSV and others interpret (as TEV) "be like a dream," that is quickly gone. Many suggestions are made for correcting the text.

We are like weeds that sprout in the morning: the meaning of the Hebrew is not clear. Many translators connect "in the morning" with what precedes, and others suggest textual changes. The word translated "weeds" may mean "grass" (RSV). The word "sprout" may have the meaning "pass away."

90.6 TEV	RSV
that grow and burst into bloom,	in the morning it flourishes and is renewed;
then dry up and die in the evening.	in the evening it fades and withers.

that grow and burst into bloom: the Hebrew has "in the morning," but since this is also in verse 5, TEV does not repeat. One of the verbs is the same as in verse 5 and may mean "grow" or "pass away."

90.7 TEV	RSV
We are destroyed by your anger;	For we are consumed by thy anger;
we are terrified by your fury.	by thy wrath we are over- whelmed.

destroyed: the Hebrew verb means "come to an end," "be finished." RSV translates "be consumed."

by your anger: the thought (see verse 8) is that God's anger about human sinfulness is what makes human life so short.

90.8 TEV	RSV
You place our sins before you,	Thou hast set our iniquities before thee,
our secret sins where you can see them.	our secret sins in the light of thy countenance.

place...before you: where they can be clearly seen and condemned. where you can see them: literally "in the light of your face" (see RSV), but this is figurative language.

90.9 TEV	RSV
Our life is cut short by your anger;	For all our days pass away under thy wrath,
it fades away like a whisper.	our years come to an end^f like a sigh.

^{f}Syr: Heb *we bring our years to an end*

90.9

Our life: the Hebrew has "our days...our years" (RSV), but this
means the total time of a person's life.
is cut short: literally "slip away," "pass away" (RSV).
fades away: the Hebrew has "we end," but there seems to be no
reason to alter the text, as RSV has done. The point is that life comes
to an end for all of us, that is, all of us complete (live out) our
years.

90.10	TEV	RSV
	Seventy years is all we have—	The years of our life are three-score and ten,
	eighty years, if we are strong;	or even by reason of strength fourscore;
	yet all they bring us is trouble and sorrow;	yet their span^g is but toil and trouble;
	life is soon over, and we are gone.	they are soon gone, and we fly away.

^{g}Cn Compare Gk Syr Jerome Tg: Heb
pride

Seventy years is all we have: the Hebrew has "the days (number) of
our years (of life) in them are seventy years." This is complicated, but
the meaning is clear: the length of life is seventy years.
if we are strong: literally "in strengths" (see RSV), but the
meaning is not certain, perhaps "at the most."
all they bring us: the m aning of the Hebrew is not certain, perhaps "their pride," "their hurry," but others change the text to say
"their great number," "their span" (RSV). In any case, the sense seems
to be "the years, whether long or short, bring only..."
trouble and sorrow: the two Hebrew words have similar meanings,
"toil, trouble (RSV), evil, sorrow, difficulty."
we are gone: the Hebrew has "we fly away," but the emphasis seems
to be on the disappearing rather than upon any view of the method of
departure at death.

90.11	TEV	RSV
	Who has felt the full power of your anger?	Who considers the power of thy anger,
	Who knows what fear your fury can bring?	and thy wrath according to the fear of thee?

has felt: the Hebrew has "knows," but in the sense of having ex-
perienced rather than considering (RSV). The rhetorical question may
need to be expressed directly in some languages: "No one has ever felt
your full anger." The point seems to be that the anger of God is so
powerful that human beings need to consider the shortness of life (verse
12).
Who knows what fear your fury can bring: the meaning of the Hebrew
(literally "and as your fear [or, fear of you] your anger") is not clear

and translations differ widely, even when no textual change is proposed. The translator is advised to follow one of the standard translations.

90.12	TEV	RSV

<table>
<tr><td>Teach us how short our
life is,
so that we may become
wise.</td><td>So teach us to number our
days
that we may get a heart
of wisdom.</td></tr>
</table>

how short our life is: this is the meaning of "to count our days" (RSV).

so that we may become wise: literally "and we will bring (or obtain) a heart of wisdom," but this means become wise, that is, know reverence for God.

90.13	TEV	RSV

<table>
<tr><td>How much longer will your
anger last?
Have pity, O LORD, on
your servants!</td><td>Return, O LORD! How long?
Have pity on thy servants!</td></tr>
</table>

How much longer...last?: the Hebrew "Return...how long" (RSV) has the meaning "How much longer will it be before you change from anger to kindness?" or "How much longer will you be angry with us?"

LORD: in English this word of address fits better in the second line than the first, but this will depend on individual language usage. In some languages the word would have to come at the beginning of the verse.

your servants: this refers to the speakers. In many languages one would have to say "have pity on us your servants" (see verse 16).

90.14	TEV	RSV

<table>
<tr><td>Fill us each morning with
your constant love,
so that we may sing and
be glad all our life.</td><td>Satisfy us in the morning
with thy steadfast love,
that we may rejoice and be
glad all our days.</td></tr>
</table>

all our life: the Hebrew "all our days" (RSV) refers to the total number of days that make up a life.

90.15	TEV	RSV

<table>
<tr><td>Give us now as much hap-
piness as the sadness
you gave us
during all our years of
misery.</td><td>Make us glad as many days
as thou hast afflicted
us,
and as many years as we
have seen evil.</td></tr>
</table>

as much: the Hebrew "as many days" (RSV) could refer to the extent of the joy, but is probably to be understood of the intensity of joy.

our years of misery: literally "years we saw evil" (see RSV), but this is a Hebrew way of speaking of experiencing misfortune, suffering. The verse is rather complicated and the translator may find it wise to restructure: "You gave us sadness during all our years of misery; now give us that much happiness."

90.16 TEV	RSV

Let us, your servants, see
    your mighty deeds;
let our descendants see
    your glorious might.
	Let thy work be manifest to
	    thy servants,
	and thy glorious power to
	    their children.

see: in the sense of experience, participate in your saving power. The active is more suitable in English than the passive "be manifest" (RSV).

descendants: the Hebrew has "sons," but the word is frequently used for descendants, both male and female. Note RSV "children."

90.17 TEV	RSV

LORD our God, may your
    blessings be with us.
Give us success in all
    we do!
	Let the favor of the Lord
	    our God be upon us,
	and establish thou the
	    work of our hands
	    upon us,
	yea, the work of our hands
	    establish thou it.

LORD our God: in English, since the prayer is to the LORD, it is necessary to take these as words of address rather than as third person, "blessing of the LORD our God" (see RSV).

blessings: the Hebrew word means "kindness," "goodness," and one, may translate "we pray that you will bless our lives" or "be kind to us."

Give us success in all we do: the Hebrew repeats the line, possibly for emphasis, shown in different ways in different languages. Note the exclamation mark in TEV. Hebrew poetry very often repeats ideas, but usually in somewhat different words. Repetition in identical words is not so frequent.

P S A L M   91

SECTION HEADING

God Our Protector: "God Protects His People."

91.1   TEV
     Whoever goes to the LORD
          for safety,
     whoever remains under the
          protection of the
          Almighty,

              RSV
     He who dwells in the shelter
          of the Most High,
     who abides in the shadow of
          the Almighty,

     goes to the LORD for safety: the Hebrew "lives in the hiding place
of the Most High" (see RSV) is a figure of the refuge provided in the
Temple for one who has gone there for protection.
     remains under the protection of the Almighty: literally "spends
the night in the shadow of the Almighty" (see RSV), which has the same
meaning as line 1 of the verse. The word "shadow" may refer to the wings
of the winged creatures overshadowing the Covenant Box.

91.2   TEV
     can say to him,
     "You are my defender and
          protector.
     You are my God; in you
          I trust."

              RSV
     will say to the LORD, "My
          refuge and my fortress;
     my God, in whom I trust."

     can say to him: the standard Hebrew text has "I say to the LORD,"
but most translations have "he says," with the Greek translation. Note
RSV "will say," with the same text.
     You are my defender and protector: that is, "you protect me and
keep me safe."
     in you I trust: that is, "I trust (or, depend) upon you."

91.3   TEV
     He will keep you safe from
          all hidden dangers
     and from all deadly
          diseases.

              RSV
     For he will deliver you from
          the snare of the fowler
     and from deadly pestilence;

     keep you safe: the Hebrew has "rescue you," but the basic sense is
protection rather than rescue (after having come into danger). The "you"
(singular) that begins here and continues through verse 13 seems to
refer to the person referred to in verses 1 and 2, that is, the one who
trusts the LORD for protection.
     all hidden dangers: the Hebrew has "the bird-catchers trap" (see
RSV), but the use is figurative, "all the things that catch you as traps
catch birds." In many languages, unless trapping birds is known, it may
be necessary to drop the figure as TEV has done. In other languages it
may be possible to translate "from all the traps that people lay for
you."
     deadly diseases: the Hebrew "the plague of destruction" (RSV "deadly
pestilence") means "the plague that kills." The same Hebrew word for
"plague" occurs in verse 6, and some scholars give the word here different vowels so as to mean "the word that destroys," meaning false accusations and plots.

91.4

TEV	RSV
He will cover you with his wings; you will be safe in his care; his faithfulness will protect and defend you.	he will cover you with his pinions, and under his wings you will find refuge; his faithfulness is a shield and buckler.

cover you with his wings...care: literally "he will cover you with his wings and you will find safety under his wings" (see RSV), but the two statements are figurative statements of one idea: he will protect you.

you will be safe in his care: that is, "He will take care of you and keep you safe (or, you will be safe)."

his faithfulness will: that is, "he is faithful and will..." or "you can depend on him to..."

will protect and defend you: the Hebrew has "is a shield and a wall (or, small shield)." The meaning of the last word is not certain. RSV translates it as "buckler," that is, "a small round shield." In any case, the figurative language clearly means "protect and defend."

91.5

TEV	RSV
You need not fear any dangers at night or sudden attacks during the day	You will not fear the terror of the night, nor the arrow that flies by day,

any dangers at night: the Hebrew may have reference to night demons or to general dangers.

sudden attacks: literally "the arrow that flies," but this will mean an attack if the words are taken literally, or perhaps in a figurative sense, "danger from enemies" (whether human or demonic).

91.6

TEV	RSV
or the plagues that strike in the dark or the evils that kill in daylight.	nor the pestilence that stalks in darkness, nor the destruction that wastes at noonday.

plagues: see verse 3. Some understand the reference to be to demonic powers, but it may mean bubonic plague or some similar disease.

evils: the Hebrew (literally "sting") probably refers to some disease or to a demon. RSV "destruction" may be too general.

91.7

TEV	RSV
A thousand may fall dead beside you, ten thousand all around you, but you will not be harmed.	A thousand may fall at your side, ten thousand at your right hand; but it will not come near you.

<u>fall dead</u>: in war or from disease.

91.8	TEV	RSV
	You will look and see how the wicked are punished.	You will only look with your eyes and see the recompense of the wicked.

<u>how the wicked are punished</u>: the Hebrew has "the repayment of the wicked" (RSV "the recompense of the wicked"), that is, how the wicked are repaid for their wickedness, which means how they are punished. One might translate "how the LORD punishes his wicked people."

91.9	TEV	RSV
	You have made the LORD your^x defender, the Most High your protector,	Because you have made the LORD your refuge,^h the Most High your habitation,

^x*Probable text* your; *Hebrew* my.

^hCN: Heb *Because thou, LORD, art my refuge ; you have made*

<u>your defender</u>: the verse begins with "because," which TEV takes as connecting this verse with what follows (see "and so" in verse 10). The Hebrew has "you, LORD, are my (place of) refuge," which may be adjusted to fit the context in line with Hebrew shifts of person. The notes in RSV and TEV indicate a change in text.

<u>your protector</u>: the Hebrew word has been interpreted as "dwelling," "habitation" (RSV), but it probably means "refuge." If it is taken this way with TEV, it is not necessary to find two words for <u>defender</u> and <u>protector</u>. One may translate "The LORD, the Most High God, will defend you."

91.10	TEV	RSV
	and so no disaster will strike you, no violence will come near your home.	no evil shall befall you, no scourge come near your tent.

<u>disaster</u>: this is the meaning here of "evil" (RSV).
<u>violence</u>: the Hebrew word may refer to an attack or to a disease.
<u>your home</u>: literally "your tent," but the sense is "home."

91.11	TEV	RSV
	God will put his angels in charge of you to protect you wherever you go.	For he will give his angels charge of you to guard you in all your ways.

91.11

wherever you go: this gives the sense of "in all your ways" (RSV).

91.12   TEV   RSV
    They will hold you up   On their hands they will bear
        with their hands   you up,
    to keep you from hurting   lest you dash your foot
        your feet on the stones.   against a stone.

hold you up: that is, as a person walks. The verb may also mean "carry."
    to keep you...feet...stones: the Hebrew has "so that you will not strike your foot against a stone" (see RSV), but the sense is protection, and the words should be understood figuratively of God's protecting care.

91.13   TEV   RSV
    You will trample down   You will tread on the lion
        lions and snakes,   and the adder,
    fierce lions and poisonous   the young lion and the
        snakes.   serpent you will trample
                                           under foot.

The various animals should be understood figuratively as representing enemies and other dangers.

91.14   TEV   RSV
    God says, "I will save those   Because he cleaves to me
        who love me   in love, I will deliver
    and will protect those who   him;
        acknowledge me as LORD.   I will protect him, because
                                           he knows my name.

God says: it is clear from the context that God is now speaking and the reader needs to be alerted to this change. Note also that TEV uses the plural in these verses for people in general, a usage that suits English style better than the singular.
    acknowledge me: the Hebrew has "knows my name" (RSV), but this verb often has the sense of "confess," and "my name" is a way of speaking of the person of God, not just the name by which he is called.

91.15   TEV   RSV
    When they call to me, I   When he calls to me, I will
        will answer them;   answer him;
    when they are in trouble,   I will be with him in
        I will be with them.   trouble,
    I will rescue them and   I will rescue him and
        honor them.   honor him.

call: that is, pray, ask for help.

be with them: this has the sense of "be there to help," not just
accompaniment.

91.16   TEV   RSV
  I will reward them with   With long life I will
    long life;   satisfy him,
  I will save them."   and show him my salvation.

    save them: the Hebrew has "cause him to see (experience) my salva-
tion" (see RSV).

                    P S A L M   95

SECTION HEADING

    A Song of Praise: "A Call to Praise and Obey the LORD."

    The psalm divides into two parts: verses 1-7c are a call to wor-
ship and verses 7d-11 contain a warning against disobedience.

95.1   TEV   RSV
  Come, let us praise the   O come, let us sing to the
    LORD!   LORD;
  Let us sing for joy to   let us make a joyful noise
    God, who protects us!   to the rock of our
                      salvation!

    Come: the Hebrew verb means "go, come, walk," but it is used in
command as an invitation to participate. The idea of motion may be
involved (for example, an invitation to pilgrims to move toward the
Temple), but more likely it has the general sense of "join in" as we
worship, and it is spoken to all of God's people.
    praise: the Hebrew verb has the meaning "shout for joy," but the
underlying idea is to express joy to the LORD because of what he is,
that is, praise him.
    sing for joy: the Hebrew verb means "shout" and has a meaning very
similar to the first verb.
    who protects us: the literal "the rock of our salvation" (RSV)
means "the rock that saves us," but the reference is to the LORD, and
the nonfigurative meaning is "the LORD protects us."

95.2   TEV   RSV
  Let us come before him with   Let us come into his presence
    thanksgiving   with thanksgiving;
  and sing joyful songs of   let us make a joyful noise
    praise.   to him with songs of praise!

come before him: literally "come in front of his face (his presence)"; the Hebrew means to enter the Temple (where God appears to his people).

with thanksgiving...songs of praise: the two Hebrew words have much the same meaning. The "with" may have to be expressed more clearly in some languages, for example, "let us sing songs of thanksgiving and praise as we come before him," that is, "as we worship him," "come into his presence," or "enter his Temple."

95.3	TEV	RSV
	For the LORD is a mighty God,	For the LORD is a great God,
	a mighty king over all the gods.	and a great King above all gods.

over all the gods: the thought is not that God is higher physically, but that he reigns over and controls all other gods.

95.4	TEV	RSV
	He rules over the whole earth,	In his hand are the depths of the earth;
	from the deepest caves to the highest hills.	the heights of the mountains are his also.

He rules over: literally "in his hand are...are his also" (RSV), but this is a figurative way of speaking of the fact that he owns and controls the world.

the whole earth: although these words are not in the Hebrew text, they are necessary if the reader is to understand that the reference to depths and heights is intended to include the whole world.

deepest caves: the Hebrew word occurs only here and probably means "the unexplored depths" of the earth (see RSV); it may refer to deep caves or to the world of the dead. A textual variant is read by one Hebrew manuscript and the Greek translation, "the far places," and this is accepted by some.

the highest hills: this may possibly refer to the ancient thought that the gods lived on the tops of mountains.

95.5	TEV	RSV
	He rules over the sea, which he made;	The sea is his, for he made it;
	the land also, which he himself formed.	for his hands formed the dry land.

rules over the sea: literally "the sea is his" (RSV), but see verse 4 for the idea of "own and control."

he himself formed: the Hebrew has "his hands formed" (RSV), but this is a way of saying that he did it personally, not that the literal hands of God made the dry land. See Genesis 1.9. The Hebrew verb is the same as that used in Genesis 2.7.

95.6

TEV	RSV
Come, let us bow down and worship him; let us kneel before the LORD, our Maker!	O come, let us worship and bow down, let us kneel before the LORD, our Maker!

bow down...worship...kneel: the Hebrew verbs all refer to bodily actions (prostrating oneself, bowing, kneeling) that are symbolic of one's attitude of respect and worship.

95.7

TEV	RSV
He is our God; we are the people he cares for, the flock for which he provides. Listen today to what he says:	For he is our God, and we are the people of his pasture, and the sheep of his hand. O that today you would hearken to his voice!

the people he cares for: literally "the people of his grazing place," that is, the people he takes care of in his pasture.

the flock for which he provides: the Hebrew "the flock (of sheep and goats) of his hand" means "the flock that he controls, protects, and cares for." There is a textual problem in the verse, and some follow one Hebrew manuscript and one ancient translation that have "we are his people and the flock of his pasture; (know) his hand." In some languages the figure which identifies people with sheep led by a shepherd may not be possible, and one may have to drop the image and speak of God's care and protection.

Listen today to what he says: this introduces the second part of the psalm. The Hebrew is literally "today that you would hear his voice (message)" (see RSV), but this is a Hebrew way of expressing a wish and means "I wish that today you would listen to what he says." TEV has found it easier to express this as a command, while RSV has retained an older form for expressing a wish.

95.8

TEV	RSV
"Don't be stubborn, as your ancestors were at Meribah, as they were that day in the desert at Massah.	Harden not your hearts, as at Meribah, as on the day at Massah in the wilderness,

Don't be stubborn: this is the meaning of the literal "do not make your hearts hard" (see RSV).

as your ancestors were at Meribah: in the Hebrew "ancestors" (literally "fathers") does not occur until verse 9, but the stubbornness at Meribah and Massah was that of their ancestors, and that should be made clear in English and many other languages by identifying the participants at their first mention. For the incidents, see Exodus 17.1-7; Numbers 20.1-13; Deuteronomy 6.16; 33.8.

95.9

TEV	RSV
There they put me to the test and tried me, although they had seen what I did for them.	when your fathers tested me, and put me to the proof, though they had seen my work.

put me to the test and tried me: the two Hebrew verbs have much the same meaning. The people "tested" the LORD by asking him to prove that he still cared for them, even though they had seen the many miracles he had performed. Note that tried is not to be understood in the legal sense of a trial. The Hebrew word was used of testing metals to see if they were genuine.

95.10

TEV	RSV
For forty years I was disgusted with those people. I said, 'How disloyal they are! They refuse to obey my commands.'	For forty years I loathed that generation and said, "They are a people who err in heart, and they do not regard my ways."

was disgusted with: the Hebrew verb has the sense of "detest," "loathe" (RSV), "dislike intensely."
disloyal: the Hebrew has "wandering off in heart," but this has the meaning "no longer follow the LORD in their hearts," "become rebellious against the LORD."
refuse to obey my commands: literally "do not know my ways," that is, "do not choose to walk in my ways," "refuse to do what I want them to do."

95.11

TEV	RSV
I was angry and made a solemn promise: 'You will never enter the land where I would have given you rest.'"	Therefore I swore in my anger that they should not enter my rest.

made a solemn promise: that is, "made a vow," "took an oath," "solemnly promised," RSV "swore."
the land where I would have given you rest: the Hebrew has "my rest" (RSV), but this means "the resting place I was going to give you," that is, the promised land. The sense is "I will not let you enter the land and be at rest" or "...live in peace."

P S A L M   96

SECTION HEADING

God the Supreme King: "The LORD is King."

There is no Hebrew title for the psalm. The text of the psalm is also found in 1 Chronicles 16.23-33 with some variations, and it is generally assumed that the author of Chronicles has borrowed and used the psalm. A translation should reflect the similarities and the differences between the two texts.

96.1

TEV	RSV
Sing a new song to the LORD! Sing to the LORD, all the world!	O sing to the LORD a new song; sing to the LORD, all the earth!

a new song: this probably refers to the psalm itself.
Sing to the LORD: this is a command, and one may translate "The whole world must sing to the LORD!"

96.2

TEV	RSV
Sing to the LORD, and praise him! Proclaim every day the good news that he has saved us.	Sing to the LORD, bless his name; tell of his salvation from day to day.

praise him: literally "bless his name," but to bless the name of the LORD means to praise him for what he is. When "bless" is used in this way, the sense is "give thanks for, praise," and "name" has the sense "person," "character."
every day: this is the sense of "from day to day."
Proclaim...the good news: the Hebrew verb means "bring good news," "make known."
that he has saved us: the Hebrew has "his salvation" (RSV), which TEV has understood as "the salvation he has brought to Israel (us)," which makes sense as parallel with "his glory" and "his mighty deeds." In some languages it may be necessary to say "saved us from our enemies." It is possible, however, that the meaning is "he will save us," "he has the power to save us."

96.3

TEV	RSV
Proclaim his glory to the nations, his mighty deeds to all peoples.	Declare his glory among the nations, his marvelous works among all the peoples!

    <u>Proclaim</u>: the Hebrew verb "make known," "tell," "declare" (RSV) is similar in meaning to the verb used in verse 2.

    <u>his glory</u>: that is, "his greatness," but there is in the word something of the idea that the LORD reveals himself in his actions of saving Israel.

    <u>his mighty deeds</u>: the Hebrew word is used of the wonderful things the LORD does to save his people, for example, the wonders he performed in saving them from Egypt.

96.4 TEV	RSV
The LORD is great and is to be highly praised; he is to be honored more than all the gods.	For great is the LORD, and greatly to be praised; he is to be feared above all gods.

    <u>honored</u>: literally "feared." The Hebrew verb expresses the idea of "stand in awe of," "have reverence for." If "fear" is used in translation, care should be taken to emphasize "awe" and "respect" rather than simply the idea of fear that God will punish.

    <u>all the gods</u>: this refers to the gods of other nations, and it may be better to introduce the idea here rather than in verse 5. One would read "the gods of all other nations. Their (or, Those) gods are only idols."

96.5 TEV	RSV
The gods of all other nations are only idols, but the LORD created the heavens.	For all the gods of the peoples are idols; but the LORD made the heavens.

    <u>idols</u>: the Hebrew word means "worthless," "nobody," and is a derogatory way of speaking of pagan gods. But the word does not deny the existence of pagan gods; it denies that they have any power. In contrast God is the creator.

96.6 TEV	RSV
Glory and majesty surround him; power and beauty fill his Temple.	Honor and majesty are before him; strength and beauty are in his sanctuary.

    <u>Glory and majesty</u>: the attributes of the king. See 45.3. It may be necessary to translate "the Lord is glorious and majestic."

    <u>power and beauty</u>: attributes associated with the presence of the LORD in his Temple, whether the earthly Temple or the heavenly dwelling place. In some languages it will not be possible to speak of the abstracts "power" and "beauty" filling the Temple. It will be better to say "the Lord is powerful and beautiful in his Temple."

96.7   TEV

    Praise the LORD, all people
        on earth;
      praise his glory and
        might.

           RSV

    Ascribe to the LORD, O families
        of the peoples,
    ascribe to the LORD glory and
        strength!

    Praise: the Hebrew word means "give," "present," "offer," but "offer glory to the LORD" has the sense of "praise the LORD for his glory." One might also translate "proclaim the glory of the LORD."

    all people on earth: the Hebrew "families of the peoples" (RSV), but this is a way of referring to the people of the world in their national or racial groupings.

96.8   TEV

    Praise the LORD's glorious
        name;
      bring an offering and come
        into his Temple.

           RSV

    Ascribe to the LORD the glory
        due his name;
    bring an offering, and come
        into his courts!

    the LORD's glorious name: the Hebrew has "the glory of his name," but this pattern often has the same sense as a noun-adjective combination in English. The meaning of "name" is that of the character and quality of the LORD himself.

    offering: the Hebrew word is general and may refer to a grain offering or an animal sacrifice.

96.9   TEV

    Bow down before the Holy One
        when he appears;^l
      tremble before him, all the
        earth!

           RSV

    Worship the LORD in holy
        array;
    tremble before him, all
        the earth!

^lwhen he appears; *or* in garments of worship.

    the Holy One when he appears: as can be seen from the note in TEV, there is some uncertainty about the meaning of the Hebrew. The Hebrew means literally something like this: "bow down to the LORD in the appearance (or, ornament) of holiness." It is possible that this means "worship the LORD in holy garments," that is, "in clothing fit for worship." That seems to be the meaning of RSV "in holy array." But more recent evidence about the meaning of "appearance, ornament" seems to indicate that the more likely meaning is "worship the LORD when his holiness appears," that is, "worship the Holy One (the Holy LORD) when he reveals himself."

    tremble before him: the Hebrew verb means "writhe," "twist," and may be taken to mean "tremble (with fear)" or possibly "dance."

96.10	TEV	RSV

<table>
<tr><td>
Say to all the nations,
  "The LORD is king!
The earth is set firmly
  in place and cannot
  be moved;
  he will judge the peoples
  with justice."
</td><td>
Say among the nations, "The
  LORD reigns!
Yea, the world is established,
  it shall never be moved;
he will judge the peoples
  with equity."
</td></tr>
</table>

is set firmly in place: this is the meaning of the Hebrew. Some translations follow the Greek text and change to active, "He (the LORD) has set firmly in place," but this is clearly what the Hebrew means in any case.

96.11	TEV	RSV

<table>
<tr><td>
Be glad, earth and sky!
  Roar, sea, and every
    creature in you;
</td><td>
Let the heavens be glad,
  and let the earth
    rejoice;
let the sea roar, and
  all that fills it;
</td></tr>
</table>

Be glad: this translates two Hebrew verbs that have much the same meaning.
Roar: the Hebrew verb means "storm," but here is thought of as "produce a joyful noise." If in the receptor language it is not possible to personify inanimate things, one may have to translate in other ways, for example, "life on the earth and the movement of stars in the sky is like people rejoicing; and the noise the sea makes in a storm is like a shout of joy."

96.12	TEV	RSV

<table>
<tr><td>
be glad, fields, and every-
  thing in you!
The trees in the woods will
  shout for joy
</td><td>
let the field exult, and
  everything in it!
Then shall all the trees of
  the wood sing for joy
</td></tr>
</table>

will shout for joy: the Hebrew has "then will shout for joy," that is, when the LORD comes (verse 13), but it is possible to understand this verb as a command, "shout for joy," like the other verbs in verses 11 and 12.

96.13	TEV	RSV

<table>
<tr><td>
when the LORD comes to
  rule the earth.
He will rule the peoples of
  the world
with justice and fairness.
</td><td>
before the LORD, for he
  comes,
for he comes to judge the
  earth.
He will judge the world with
  righteousness,
and the peoples with his
  truth.
</td></tr>
</table>

when the LORD comes: TEV has reduced the Hebrew repetition, "when he comes, when he comes" (see RSV).

to rule: the Hebrew verb may be translated "to judge," but here the LORD is coming as king to govern the world and not just to judge it. The Hebrew verb is frequently used in the more general sense. See, for example, the rulers in the Book of Judges.

with justice and fairness: this is the sense of the literal "with righteousness and truth" (see RSV).

P S A L M 100

SECTION HEADING

A Hymn of Praise[q]: "A Call to Praise God."

TEV	RSV
[q]HEBREW TITLE: *A psalm of thanks-giving.*	A Psalm for the thank offering.

The Hebrew title, found in the footnote of TEV, is "a psalm of thanksgiving" or "a psalm for the thank offering," but in verse 4 the same Hebrew word means "thanksgiving."

100.1 TEV	RSV
Sing to the LORD, all the world!	Make a joyful noise to the LORD, all the lands![n]

[n]Heb *land* or *earth*

Sing to the LORD: that is, "sing the praises of the LORD," "sing to honor the LORD."

100.2 TEV	RSV
Worship the LORD with joy; come before him with happy songs!	Serve the LORD with gladness! Come into his presence with singing!

Worship: literally "serve," but the meaning of service in this context is primarily "worship," although one may prefer to choose, if this is possible, a word that could include worship in the Temple and also a life lived in service.

before him: literally "before his face, his presence," but the point is that the worshiper comes into the Temple, where the LORD is to be found in a special way.

100.3 TEV	RSV

Acknowledge that the
    LORD is God.
He made us, and we
    belong to him;
we are his people,
    we are his flock.
	Know that the LORD is
	    God!
	It is he that made us, and
	    we are his;^{O}
	we are his people, and the
	    sheep of his pasture.

^{O}Another reading is *and not we
ourselves*

Acknowledge: Hebrew "Know" (RSV), but the verb has also the sense of "recognize," "acknowledge," "confess by saying (as in a creed)."

and we belong to him: this is almost certainly what the Hebrew means, although another form of the text reads "and not we ourselves," as shown in the RSV footnote.

we are his flock: it may be necessary to clarify the figure ("the LORD takes care of us as a shepherd takes care of his flock") or drop it ("the LORD takes care of us").

100.4 TEV	RSV

Enter the Temple gates with
    thanksgiving;
go into its courts with
    praise.
Give thanks to him and
    praise him.
	Enter his gates with
	    thanksgiving,
	and his courts with
	    praise!
	Give thanks to him,
	    bless his name!

Enter...with thanksgiving: that is, "sing songs of thanksgiving as you enter."

100.5 TEV	RSV

The LORD is good;
    his love is eternal
and his faithfulness
    lasts forever.
	For the LORD is good;
	    his steadfast love endures
	        for ever,
	and his faithfulness to all
	        generations.

his love: the Hebrew verb expresses the thought that the LORD cares for his people as he promised in his covenant with them. Often it will be clearer to translate "he will never stop loving us."

his faithfulness: the LORD remains faithful to the promises he has made to his people, that is, "he will always be faithful to (his covenant with) us."

P S A L M   103

SECTION HEADING

The Love of God^v

TEV	RSV
^{v}HEBREW TITLE: *By David.*	A Psalm of David.

The Hebrew title, in the footnote of TEV, is simply "by David" or "for David."

103.1 TEV	RSV
Praise the LORD, my soul! All my being, praise his holy name!	Bless the LORD, O my soul; and all that is within me, bless his holy name!

Praise: the Hebrew "Bless" (RSV) has the sense of "tell of the greatness of," that is, "praise."
my soul: the psalmist speaks to himself. The Hebrew word "soul" means "life," "being," as a gift from God. In many languages it may not be possible to speak to oneself in this way. One may translate "I want my whole life (or, being) to praise the LORD."

103.2 TEV	TEV
Praise the LORD, my soul, and do not forget how kind he is.	Bless the LORD, O my soul, and forget not all his benefits,

how kind he is: the Hebrew has "his (good) deeds," that is, "the good (kind) things he has done." RSV has "his benefits."

103.3 TEV	RSV
He forgives all my sins and heals all my diseases.	who forgives all your iniquity, who heals all your diseases,

He forgives: literally "the one forgiving," that is, "who forgives" (RSV), but in English and other languages the single sentence running through verse 5 is extremely complex, and it is much wiser to begin a new sentence here.
my sins: the Hebrew has "your sins," where "your" refers to the psalmist's soul (verse 1), but this is very difficult, particularly in languages which will have problems with the psalmist speaking to himself as "you." It seems wiser to shift to first person.

103.4 TEV	RSV
He keeps me from the grave	who redeems your life from the Pit,

[105]

and blesses me with love and mercy.	who crowns you with steadfast love and mercy,

keeps me from the grave: the Hebrew has "redeems (rescues) your (my) life from the pit (the grave or the world of the dead)." Most interpreters understand this to mean that the LORD protects and delivers from death, but some take it to mean resurrection.

blesses: literally "crowns," "puts a crown on." Here the thought is that the LORD will honor the psalmist by putting a crown (symbol of victory) made of love and mercy on his head. In languages where such figurative usages are not possible, one may have to drop the symbol and say, for example, "the LORD highly honors me by giving me his love and mercy," or "blesses me with..."

103.5 TEV	RSV
He fills my life*w* with good things, so that I stay young and strong like an eagle.	who satisfies you with good as long as you live*q* so that your youth is renewed like the eagle's.
	*q*Heb uncertain

wProbable text my life; Hebrew unclear.

fills: the Hebrew verb has the meaning "satisfy," "fills."

my life: as the note in TEV shows, there is some difficulty in understanding the meaning of the Hebrew word. It seems to mean "my ornaments," but this makes no sense. The King James Version "my mouth" cannot be correct. Some have proposed "my vitality," "my eternity," "my strength," "my desire." TEV follows those who change the text to mean "as long as you live" (RSV) and interprets as "my life."

stay young and strong: the Hebrew "my youth is renewed" (see RSV) has the sense that old age does not come.

103.6 TEV	RSV
The LORD judges in favor of the oppressed and gives them their rights.	The LORD works vindication and justice for all who are oppressed.

judges in favor of...gives them their rights: the two Hebrew verbs have much the same meaning. The LORD gives justice to those who have been treated unjustly.

103.7 TEV	RSV
He revealed his plans to Moses and let the people of Israel see his mighty deeds.	He made known his ways to Moses, his acts to the people of Israel.

his plans: the Hebrew "his ways" could refer to the way God had acted in the past, but it is more likely that it refers to what he is going to do, that is, his plans.

his mighty deeds: the Hebrew has "his deeds," but what is in focus is the mighty acts he did to save his people from their enemies. One might translate "the mighty things he had done."

103.8	TEV	RSV
	The LORD is merciful and loving, slow to become angry and full of constant love.	The LORD is merciful and gracious, slow to anger and abounding in steadfast love.

full of constant love: this refers to the faithful care he provides for those who obey his covenant. One might translate "his love has no limits" or "he never stops loving his people."

103.9	TEV	RSV
	He does not keep on rebuking; he is not angry forever.	He will not always chide, nor will he keep his anger for ever.

keep on rebuking: the Hebrew verb has the sense "make accusations in the law court."

103.10	TEV	RSV
	He does not punish us as we deserve or repay us according to our sins and wrongs.	He does not deal with us according to our sins, nor requite us according to our iniquities.

repay: the Hebrew verb means "to deal with" (RSV), "reward," but here is used in the negative sense, "punish."

103.11	TEV	RSV
	As high as the sky is above the earth, so great is his love for those who honor him.	For as the heavens are high above the earth, so great is his steadfast love toward those who fear him;

As high...so great: the construction is difficult; it may be necessary to rearrange: "his love is very great...; it is so great that it could be compared to how high the sky is above the earth."

so great: the height of the sky is compared with the greatness of the love of the LORD, but some change the Hebrew to "so high." In any case, we are dealing with a kind of figurative language which explains the greatness of God's love.

103.11

who honor him: literally "who fear him." See 96.4.

103.12   TEV   RSV
   As far as the east is   as far as the east is from
      from the west,   the west,
   so far does he remove   so far does he remove our
      our sins from us.   transgressions from us.

so far does he remove: the Hebrew verb has a meaning of distance,
"move away," but it must be understood that this is an image for the
forgiveness of sins.

103.13   TEV   RSV
   As a father is kind to   As a father pities his
      his children,   children,
   so the LORD is kind to   so the LORD pities those
      those who honor him.   who fear him.

is kind: the Hebrew verb has the meaning of "show love," "show
compassion," that is, "deal kindly with." The LORD's mercy is compared
to that of a kind father. The RSV "pities" gives the wrong meaning in
modern English.
   who honor him: literally "who fear him." See verse 11, where the
same verb is used.

103.14   TEV   RSV
   He knows what we are   For he knows our frame;
      made of;   he remembers that we
   he remembers that we   are dust.
      are dust.

what we are made of: the Hebrew word means "what is shaped or
made." One might translate "how we are made," "how weak we are." RSV
"our frame" is difficult.
   dust: the same Hebrew word is used in Genesis 2.7, where TEV
translates it "soil." The psalmist is recalling that God formed man
from the ground.

103.15   TEV   RSV
   As for us, our life is   As for man, his days are
      like grass.   like grass;
   We grow and flourish like   he flourishes like a
      a wild flower;   flower of the field;

our life is like grass: literally "his days (man's days) are like
grass." The point, of course, is that just as grass is very temporary,
humans are here for just a short time.
   grow and flourish: the Hebrew has "sprout," "bloom," but humans

are being compared to a flower, "just as a flower blooms, so human life develops"; then it suddenly comes to an end.

<u>wild flower</u>: this is the meaning of "flower of the field" (RSV).

103.16	TEV	RSV
	then the wind blows on it,	for the wind passes over it,
	and it is gone—	and it is gone,
	no one sees it again.	and its place knows it no
		more.

<u>no one sees it again</u>: literally "its (his) place knows it (him) no longer," that is to say, "it is completely gone," "no trace is left."

103.17	TEV	RSV
	But for those who honor the	But the steadfast love of
	LORD, his love lasts	the LORD is from ever-
	forever,	lasting to everlasting
	and his goodness endures	upon those who fear him,
	for all generations	and his righteousness to
		children's children,

<u>honor</u>: literally "fear." See verses 11 and 13.

<u>love</u>: the Hebrew word refers to the steadfast, constant love and care that the LORD shows to his people.

<u>lasts forever</u>: this is the meaning of "is from everlasting to everlasting" (RSV).

<u>all generations</u>: this is the meaning of the literal "to children's children," that is, "generation after generation."

103.18	TEV	RSV
	of those who are true to	to those who keep his
	his covenant	covenant
	and who faithfully obey	and remember to do his
	his commands.	commandments.

<u>true to his covenant</u>: "keep (guard) his covenant" (RSV), that is, obey the commands that are given as the people's reponsibility to the covenant.

<u>faithfully obey</u>: Hebrew "remember to do" (RSV), but this is a way of expressing "are careful to do," that is, "obey carefully."

103.19	TEV	RSV
	The LORD placed his throne	The LORD has established his
	in heaven;	throne in the heavens,
	he is king over all.	and his kingdom rules over
		all.

<u>his throne</u>: this is a symbol of his kingship. In languages which

do not have this symbol, it may be necessary to translate "the LORD reigns from heaven."

103.20	TEV	RSV
	Praise the LORD, you strong and mighty angels, who obey his commands, who listen to what he says.	Bless the LORD, O you his angels, you mighty ones who do his word, hearkening to the voice of his word!

strong and mighty angels: this is the meaning of the literal "angels, strong and mighty ones." Some manuscripts have "all his angels."

obey his commands: this is the meaning of the literal "do his word."

103.21	TEV	RSV
	Praise the LORD, all you heavenly powers, you servants of his, who do his will!	Bless the LORD, all his hosts, his ministers that do his will!

all you heavenly powers: literally "all his armies," but this refers to the heavenly armies who obey the LORD and do his bidding. One might translate "all you mighty angels in heaven."

servants: that is, "those who wait on" the LORD. Note that angels," "heavenly powers," and "servants" refer to the same group of heavenly beings, and not to three separate groups. The angels are the heavenly powers and the servants.

103.22	TEV	RSV
	Praise the LORD, all his creatures in all the places he rules. Praise the LORD, my soul!	Bless the LORD, all his works, in all places of his dominion. Bless the LORD, O my soul!

Praise the LORD, my soul: this is identical with the first line of the psalm.

PSALM   104

SECTION HEADING

In Praise of the Creator: "Praise the LORD, the Creator of the Universe," "The LORD is the Creator."

[110]

There is no Hebrew title to this psalm.

104.1

TEV	RSV
Praise the LORD, my soul! O LORD, my God, how great you are! You are clothed with majesty and glory;	Bless the LORD, O my soul! O LORD my God, thou art very great! Thou art clothed with honor and majesty,

Praise the LORD, my soul!: see 103.1, which is the same in Hebrew.
The style of the whole psalm is similar to that of 103, and many assume
that they were composed by the same author.
how great you are!: this is an emphatic way of stating what the
Hebrew has, "you are very great."
clothed with majesty and glory: this image of being clothed may
have to be dropped, for example, "you are majestic and glorious."

104.2

TEV	RSV
you cover yourself with light. You have spread out the heavens like a tent	who coverest thyself with light as with a garment, who hast stretched out the heavens like a tent,

with light: the Hebrew has "with light as with a garment (mantle)."
TEV has dropped a part of the figure, which might be expressed by "the
LORD covers himself with light just as a person covers himself with a
garment (or, blanket)."

104.3

TEV	RSV
and built your home on the waters above.^{x} You use the clouds as your chariot and ride on the wings of the wind.	who hast laid the beams of thy chambers on the waters, who makest the clouds thy chariot, who ridest on the wings of the wind,

^{x}THE WATERS ABOVE: *A reference to
the waters above the celestial
dome (Gen 1.6-7).*

built your home: literally "you constructed with beams your upper
rooms," that is, "you used beams in the construction of your home (above
the water)." Here the LORD's dwelling place in heaven is compared to a
house built above the water on piles or beams that are driven into the
ground for support.
the waters above: as the TEV note shows, the literal "on the
water" refers to the fact that God's dwelling place is above the heavenly ocean, which in Hebrew thought is held back by the sky from flood-
ing the earth (see Gen 1.6-8).

104.3

chariot: the clouds are compared to a chariot in which a king rides.
ride: the LORD is thought of as riding on the clouds and the winds
as he comes to visit the earth.
the wings of the wind: this poetic imagery compares the wind to a
bird, which uses its wings to fly. In some languages the figure may have
to be dropped and one may have to translate "he rides on the clouds and
the wind."

	104.4	TEV	RSV

104.4
TEV
You use the winds as your
   messengers
and flashes of lightning
   as your servants.

RSV
who makest the winds thy
   messengers,
fire and flame thy ministers.

messengers...servants: winds and lightning are pictured as persons
who do what the LORD commands in carrying messages and performing other
duties. Where such things cannot be thought of as persons, one may have
to translate "just as men carry the messages of kings and do what kings
command, so the wind and the lightning obey you, LORD."
flashes of lightning: literally "a flaming fire," which probably
refers to lightning, although some people take the meaning to be fire
itself. Hebrews 1.7 quotes the Greek translation of this verse, understood as flames of fire. Others change the Hebrew text to read "fire
and flame" (RSV).

104.5
TEV
You have set the earth firmly
   on its foundations,
and it will never be moved.

RSV
Thou didst set the earth on
   its foundations,
so that it should never be
   shaken.

foundations: these are the great pillars that support the earth
above the underground water, in the Hebrew view of the world. The picture in verses 5-9 is that of the creation of the world from watery
chaos (see Gen 1.2).
never be moved: in Hebrew never is expressed in a very emphatic
way. The Hebrew verb has the sense "be made to totter," "be shaken
from its foundations."

104.6
TEV
You placed the ocean over
   it like a robe,
and the water covered the
   mountains.

RSV
Thou didst cover it with the
   deep as with a garment;
the waters stood above the
   mountains.

You placed the ocean over it like a robe: this is the meaning of
the Hebrew text, but some translations make a slight change in the
Hebrew text, to say "the ocean was spread over the earth like a robe,"
and this makes excellent sense in the context. The word ocean refers to

[112]

the chaotic waters at the time of creation.

104.7   TEV

   When you rebuked the waters,
      they fled;
      they rushed away when they
         heard your shout of
         command.

                                  RSV

   At thy rebuke they fled;
      at the sound of thy thunder
         they took to flight.

    rebuked: the Hebrew word has the sense of "reproach," "threaten," but in parallel with the next line the meaning is "give a sharp command."
    your shout of command: literally "the voice of your thunder," but in the Old Testament God is said to speak in thunder. Here the voice is directed against the water.

104.8   TEV

   They flowed over the
      mountains and into
      the valleys,
    to the place you had
    made for them.

                                    RSV

   The mountains rose, the
      valleys sank down
    to the place which thou
      didst appoint for
      them.

    They flowed over the mountains: there is disagreement as to how the Hebrew of this verse is to be interpreted. TEV has understood "the waters" to be the subject of the Hebrew verb "go up," but RSV takes "the mountains" as subject. The end of the verse and verse 9, with the reference to the enclosure for the sea, make the TEV interpretation more likely (see Gen 1.6-9). The meaning would be that the water, which had covered the mountains, flowed down the mountains and through the valleys into the place that God had set for the sea.

104.9   TEV

   You set a boundary they
      can never pass,
    to keep them from covering
      the earth again.

                                    RSV

   Thou dist set a bound which
      they should not pass,
    so that they might not again
      cover the earth.

    boundary: this refers to the limits which God set for the sea, the enclosure within which the chaotic waters were to remain.

104.10   TEV

   You make springs flow in
      the valleys,
    and rivers run between
      the hills.

                                    RSV

   Thou makest springs gush
      forth in the valleys;
    they flow between the
      hills,

    in the valleys: the Hebrew may refer to the streams of water which flow from the springs in the valleys, but it seems more likely that the word refers to the stream beds or valleys through which the water flows.

104.11   TEV   RSV
    They provide water for the   they give drink to every
      wild animals;   beast of the field;
    there the wild donkeys quench   the wild asses quench their
      their thirst.   thirst.

    the wild animals: this is the meaning of the literal "all the
animals of the field" (see RSV).

104.12   TEV   RSV
    In the trees near by,   By them the birds of the air
      the birds make their   have their habitation;
      nests and sing.   they sing among the
                              branches.

    the trees: the word itself does not occur in the Hebrew, but the
context seems to require this idea. Note the reference to "branches"
(RSV).

104.13   TEV   RSV
    From the sky you send rain   From thy lofty abode thou
      on the hills,   waterest the mountains;
    and the earth is filled with   the earth is satisfied with
      your blessings.   the fruit of thy work.

    the sky: Hebrew has "your upper rooms," the same word as in verse
3. God's dwelling place is thought of as above the sky.
    you send rain: literally "you give to drink," that is, "provide
the water that is needed." In most languages it will be simpler to use
the normal expression for sending rain.
    is filled with your blessings: literally "is satisfied from the
fruit (result) of your work" (see RSV). This seems to refer to the
blessing of abundant crops, which result from the rain sent by the LORD.
It would also be possible, although perhaps less likely, to interpret
"the earth is well watered." Many suggestions have been made to change
the Hebrew text, but in following the Hebrew one might translate "and
you pour (your) blessings out on the earth and cover the earth with
crops" or "...and the earth has all the water it needs."

104.14   TEV   RSV
    You make grass grow for the   Thou dost cause the grass
      cattle   to grow for the cattle,
    and plants for man to use,   and plants for man to
    so that he can grow his crops   cultivate,[r]
                         that he may bring forth
                         food from the earth,

rOr *fodder for the animals that
serve man*

    for man to use: the Hebrew "for the service (work, cultivation) of
man" can be understood to mean "plants for man to cultivate" (RSV) or
can be understood in a more general way (TEV). In the latter sense the
line is a summary of the ideas of growing crops in the next lines. Here,
of course, man refers to mankind and not just to males.
    grow his crops: literally "cause bread to come forth from the
earth, ground," but "bread" is used frequently to refer to food in general, and "to bring food from the earth" refers to growing crops. A
normal way of speaking of growing crops should be used.

104.15	TEV	RSV

	and produce wine to make
	    him happy,
	olive oil to make him
	    cheerful,
	and bread to give him
	    strength.
		and wine to gladden the
		    heart of man,
		oil to make his face
		    shine,
		and bread to strengthen
		    man's heart.

    produce: in the Hebrew the verb of verse 14 is carried on with
wine as the object, as in RSV, but in English and other languages it
is simpler to supply a parallel verb. Here, of course, the thought is
that rain waters the earth and makes vines grow, which produce grapes,
from which wine can be made.
    to make him happy: literally "which makes glad the heart of man"
(see RSV), but the heart represents the whole well-being of man. It is
not just a part of him that is happy.
    to make him cheerful: the Hebrew "to make his face shine" (RSV)
probably has the figurative meaning that TEV has given, although the
words could be understood literally, since olive oil was rubbed on the
skin to protect it and keep it soft.
    bread: the same Hebrew word as in verse 14, which here may refer
to the production of wheat, from which bread is made, but it may have
the general meaning of "food."
    to give him strength: literally "which strengthens the heart of
man" (see to make him happy above).

104.16	TEV	RSV

	The cedars of Lebanon get
	    plenty of rain—
	the LORD's own trees, which
	    he planted.
		The trees of the LORD are
		    watered abundantly,
		the cedars of Lebanon which
		    he planted.

    The cedars of Lebanon: note that TEV has reversed the order, so
that "the trees of the LORD" would be more easily identified.
    get plenty of rain: the Hebrew has "are satisfied," which probably
refers to sufficient rain. Note RSV "are watered abundantly."

104.17	TEV	RSV
	There the birds build their nests; the storks nest in the fir trees.	In them the birds build their nests; the stork has her home in the fir trees.

storks: a description of the birds and animals mentioned in these verses can be found in Fauna and Flora of the Bible.

fir trees: the Hebrew text seems to refer to a type of tree (possibly fir or cypress), but some translations make a slight change in the text and read "on the tops of them," that is, the cedars of verse 16, and this may be correct.

104.18	TEV	RSV
	The wild goats live in the high mountains, and the rock badgers hide in the cliffs.	The high mountains are for the wild goats; the rocks are a refuge for the badgers.

rock badgers: this is a rabbit-like animal, a hyrax.

104.19	TEV	RSV
	You created the moon to mark the months; the sun knows the time to set.	Thou hast made the moon to mark the seasons; the sun knows its time for setting.

months: the Hebrew word means "appointed times," but in the lunar calendar of the Hebrews the moon showed the beginning of the months and the time for festivals.

the sun knows: if this personification cannot be expressed, one may translate "you tell the sun when to go down" or something like that. The psalmist is saying that everything is created and controlled by the LORD.

104.20	TEV	RSV
	You made the night, and in the darkness all the wild animals come out.	Thou makest darkness, and it is night, when all the beasts of the forest creep forth.

the wild animals: literally "the animals of the forest," but the meaning is quite similar to what is expressed in verse 11. The point is that at night wild animals leave their dens to hunt.

104.21	TEV	RSV
	The young lions roar while they hunt,	The young lions roar for their prey,

looking for the food that God provides.	seeking their food from God.

while they hunt: the Hebrew has "for their prey" (RSV), that is, while they hunt for other animals that they can kill, tear up, and eat.

104.22 TEV	RSV
When the sun rises, they go back and lie down in their dens.	When the sun rises, they get them away and lie down in their dens.

go back: that is, they withdraw and return to their homes (dens).

104.23 TEV	RSV
Then people go out to do their work and keep working until evening.	Man goes forth to his work and to his labor until the evening.

people: this is the meaning of the Hebrew word "man, mankind."

104.24 TEV	RSV
LORD, you have made so many things! How wisely you made them all! The earth is filled with your creatures.	O LORD, how manifold are thy works! In wisdom hast thou made them all; the earth is full of thy creatures.

you have made so many things: literally "how numerous are your works (things you have made)" (see RSV), but this is in Hebrew an emphatic way of stating what TEV translates.

How wisely: this is an English emphatic construction. One might translate "all that you made was made in wisdom," "you were very wise when you made everything."

your creatures: that is, things that you have created, although the word could possibly be understood as "your possession."

104.25 TEV	RSV
There is the ocean, large and wide, where countless creatures live, large and small alike.	Yonder is the sea, great and wide, which teems with things innumerable, living things both small and great.

countless creatures: here the Hebrew has the sense "is filled with countless living things (animals)" (see RSV), and the reference is to fish, whales, and other animals.

104.26	TEV	RSV
	The ships sail on it, and in it plays Leviathan, that sea monster which you made.ᵞ	There go the ships, and Leviathan which thou didst form to sport in it.

ᵞin it plays...made; *or* Leviathan is there, that sea monster you made to amuse you.

    in it plays Leviathan: as the TEV note shows, the Hebrew may be understood to mean "to play in it" (that is, Leviathan plays in the sea) or "to play with it" (that is, the Lord plays with Leviathan). If the second meaning is intended, the thought would be that the great dragon or sea monster was controlled by God as if it were a puppy playing in the house.

104.27	TEV	RSV
	All of them depend on you to give them food when they need it.	These all look to thee, to give them their food in due season.

    depend on you: literally "hope (or, wait) for you," that is, expect their food to come from the LORD.
    when they need it: this is what is intended by the literal "in its (right) time."

104.28	TEV	RSV
	You give it to them, and they eat it; you provide food, and they are satisfied.	When thou givest to them, they gather it up; when thou openest thy hand, they are filled with good things.

    they eat it: the Hebrew "they gather up" (see RSV) is used for getting food to eat.
    you provide: the words "you open your hand" (see RSV) emphasizes God's activity in providing food for all the animals, but a literal translation may give a false meaning, rather than emphasize the direct activity of God, as the Hebrew does.
    they are satisfied: the Hebrew "they are satisfied with good" means "they have as much food as they want to eat."

104.29	TEV	RSV
	When you turn away, they are afraid;	When thou hidest thy face, they are dismayed;

```
    when you take away your              when thou takest away their
        breath, they die                     breath, they die
    and go back to the dust              and return to their dust.
        from which they came.
```

you turn away: literally "you hide your face" (see RSV), which has the meaning "withdraw," "no longer be present to help." The "face" is a symbol of God's presence.

your breath: God gives people and animals their breath (life), and when he withdraws the breath he gives, they die. The standard Hebrew text has "their breath" (RSV), but others read "your breath," as found in the next line of the Hebrew. In either case, the meaning will be the same, "God takes away the breath that he has given them," and this may be spoken of as "their breath" or "your breath," depending on the particular emphasis. Perhaps it is best to translate "the breath you have given them."

the dust from which they came: literally "their dust," but this does not mean that they own it; rather it means the soil from which they were formed (see Gen 2.19).

104.30   TEV   RSV
    But when you give them   When thou sendest forth thy
        breath,² they are   Spirit,⁸ they are
        created;   created;
    you give new life to   and thou renewest the face
        the earth.   of the ground.

²give them breath; or send out   ⁸Or breath
  your spirit.

you give them breath: see verse 29. The Hebrew word for "breath" may also mean "wind," "spirit," and the verb translated give may also have the meaning "send." It is hard to decide here, although there is no doubt that the reference is to the creative power of God. One may place one interpretation in the text and include the other in a footnote, as TEV has done. The RSV "Spirit" may be misinterpreted to mean "the Holy Spirit" in the New Testament sense, which is extremely unlikely here.

you give new life to the earth: the verse is not dealing primarily with the original creation, but with the continuing creativity of God as successive generations are born. He gives each new creature breath. He continues to renew life on earth, and life would cease if he were not active. This is what is meant by the literal "renew the face of the ground." A literal translation would mislead the reader into thinking that the ground itself was worn out and had to be renewed.

104.31   TEV   RSV
    May the glory of the LORD   May the glory of the LORD
        last forever!   endure for ever,
    May the LORD be happy with   may the LORD rejoice in his
        what he has made!   works,
```
```

104.31

glory: the familiar word here refers to the royal splendor of God as creator (see verse 1).

be happy with what he has made: literally "be glad about his works (what he has made)," and the words probably reflect the refrain of Genesis 1, "God was pleased."

104.32	TEV	RSV
	He looks at the earth, and it trembles; he touches the mountains, and they pour out smoke.	who looks on the earth and it trembles, who touches the mountains and they smoke!

looks: the verse emphasizes the Lord's complete control of the world. He can look at or touch any part of it, and that part will be destroyed. The reference seems to be to earthquakes and volcanoes.

104.33	TEV	RSV
	I will sing to the LORD all my life; as long as I live I will sing praises to my God.	I will sing to the LORD as long as I live; I will sing praise to my God while I have being.

all my life; as long as I live: the two Hebrew expressions have essentially the same meaning, as do sing and sing praises. It may be necessary to compress: "As long as I live I will sing praises to the Lord my God."

104.34	TEV	RSV
	May he be pleased with my song, for my gladness comes from him.	May my meditation be pleasing to him, for I rejoice in the LORD.

my song: the Hebrew word means "what concerns or interests a person" and might be translated "poems," "thoughts," "meditation" (RSV), but it does seem likely that the psalmist is referring to what has been expressed in the psalm.

my gladness comes from him: literally "I am glad in the LORD," which probably means "the LORD is the source of my gladness." One may translate "the LORD makes me glad" or "...is the one who makes me glad."

104.35	TEV	RSV
	May sinners be destroyed from the earth; may the wicked be no more.	Let sinners be consumed from the earth, and let the wicked be no more!

```
Praise the LORD, my soul!          Bless the LORD, O my soul!
Praise the LORD!                   Praise the LORD!
```

sinners: the thought of the psalmist seems to be that those who
have turned away from God and do not praise him have no right to exist.
Praise the LORD: the psalm ends with the same words with which it
began (see verse 1). There is no good reason to follow the Greek translation in placing the last words at the beginning of Psalm 105.

PSALM   110

SECTION HEADING

The Lord and His Chosen King[l]: "The Priest-King," "The Lord's
Chosen King."


```
              TEV                        RSV
[l]HEBREW TITLE: A psalm by David.    A Psalm of David.
```

The Hebrew title appears in the margin of TEV. This psalm cele-
brates the enthronement of a king, but it is not known when it was
written. By the time of Jesus it was interpreted as referring to the
Messiah (see Mark 12.35-37 and the parallels). There are many problems
in the text and the interpretation of this psalm, and often the translator can do little more than guess at the original meaning.


```
110.1          TEV                        RSV
The LORD said to my lord, the     The LORD says to my lord:
    king,                           "Sit at my right hand,
 "Sit here at my right side        till I make your enemies
 until I put your enemies            your footstool."
    under your feet."
```

The LORD said: the Hebrew uses a noun form that is common in pro-
phetic speech (but found only here in the psalms), "the utterance/say-
ing of the LORD." In most translations it will be better to use a verb,
as RSV and TEV have done.
my lord, the king: it is generally agreed that the LORD speaks to
the (new) king when he addresses my lord. TEV makes this clear by identifying my lord as the king. Most translations will need to do something
like this if readers are to understand the meaning.
at my right side: in Hebrew thought, to sit at the right side means
not only to be in a place of honor, but also to have some of the authority and power of the person at whose right one sits. Here the king is
commanded or invited to sit at the right of the LORD, and that means
that the king is seen as receiving his power and authority from God. In
some languages it may be necessary to translate more directly, for example, "I give you my authority and power."

put your enemies under your feet: literally "place your enemies as a footstool under your feet." TEV has found it necessary to drop part of the figurative language, and some languages may find it necessary to express the meaning directly, "make you completely victorious over your enemies," and that is what the figurative language means.

110.2	TEV	RSV
	From Zion the LORD will extend your royal power. "Rule over your enemies," he says.	The LORD sends forth from Zion your mighty scepter. Rule in the midst of your foes!

The king is still being addressed, but the speaker is now not the LORD (as in verse 1) but the singer of the psalm.

From Zion: the word "Zion" may refer to the city of Jerusalem, as TEV has understood, or it may be understood as referring to the Temple, the dwelling place of God. In the first case it is stated that the king's rule will extend out from his capital city, and in the second (which seems more likely) it is stated that the king's power to rule is a direct gift from the LORD. In some languages it may be necessary to translate "from Jerusalem, your capital city" or "from the Temple of the LORD," if that interpretation is chosen.

will extend your royal power: literally "will send forth your mighty scepter." The scepter is a symbol of the king's power and authority to rule his people. In languages in which this symbol is not known, it may be necessary to substitute another symbol for royal authority (but this must be handled with care) or drop the symbol, as TEV has done, and speak of "kingly authority," "the right of the king to rule," or something like that. Instead of a promise or statement about the future, the Hebrew verb may be understood as a wish, "may the LORD ...," "I pray that the LORD will..."

Rule over your enemies: literally "Rule in the middle of your enemies," but that means "Rule surrounded by the enemies (that you have conquered)," and it may be better to express this in a direct way, Rule over your enemies.

he says: these words are not in the Hebrew, but they are required in English if one interprets the text to mean that the LORD speaks the command to rule, as TEV does. Otherwise the command will be understood as spoken by the singer of the psalm and would express a kind of wish, "I pray that you may rule over your enemies." In many languages it will be necessary to indicate even more clearly than English does who the speaker of verse 2 is. It seems more natural to assume that it is the psalmist throughout the verse than to assume that the first part is spoken by the psalmist and the second part by the LORD.

110.3	TEV	RSV
	On the day you fight your enemies, your people will volunteer.	Your people will offer themselves freely on the day you lead your host

Like the dew of early
    morning
  your young men will
    come to you on the
    sacred hills.^m
	upon the holy mountains.^e
	  From the womb of the morn-
	    ing
	  like dew your youth^f will
	    come to you.

^mVerse 3 in Hebrew is unclear.

^eAnother reading is *in holy array*

^fCn: Heb *the dew of your youth*

The meaning of the Hebrew in this verse is quite unclear, as the TEV note shows. A textual problem has to be faced in almost every phrase of the Hebrew, and the translator is advised to follow one translation for the whole verse.

On the day you fight your enemies: literally "on the day of your power" (the second element in the Hebrew order), but the word translated "power" may have the meaning "strength," "army," "wealth." TEV has understood the reference to be to leading the army in battle (see also RSV), but it is possible that the words refer to the day in which the unnamed person is made king. There is a further complication in that some translations change the text to read "on the day of your birth" (see NEB), but this is not recommended, even though "birth" could be understood to refer to the day the person was made king. It is probably best to follow the TEV and RSV interpretation.

your people will volunteer: the Hebrew has "your people (are) free will offerings," which is interpreted to mean "will offer themselves (as soldiers of the king)," but it is not certain that is what the Hebrew means. The Greek translation possibly reflects the original text, "with you (are) noble things," which could have the sense "you have been given king-like (or, royal) gifts (or, powers)" or even "you are surrounded by princes, or nobles (in your court)." The reference would be to the splendor of the king on the day of his enthronement.

Like the dew: the Hebrew "to you the dew" (the fifth element of the text), but there is much disagreement about the meaning; possibly "go forth as dew" or "I said of you like dew."

of early morning: literally "from the womb from (or, of) the dawn" (see RSV), but the meaning is not clear, and much will depend on how it is connected with the rest of the verse.

your young men: the Hebrew has "of your young manhood" (the last element of the text). The original text, possibly reflected in many Hebrew manuscripts and the Greek translation, may have been "I have brought you to birth." The RSV translation is a conjecture, as the footnote shows.

on the sacred hills: literally "in ornaments of holiness" (possibly meaning "in royal robes"), but many Hebrew manuscripts have "on the mountains of holiness," which may be the original text. Note RSV and the footnote.

Needless to say, the meaning of the verse is not clear. One is advised to follow any of the standard translations (with perhaps a note stating that the meaning is uncertain).

110.4	TEV	RSV

The LORD made a solemn
   promise and will not
   take it back:
"You will be a priest
   forever
in the priestly order
of Melchizedek."[n]

The LORD has sworn
   and will not change his
   mind,
"You are a priest for ever
   after the order of Melchizedek."

[n]in the priestly order of Melchizedek; *or* like Melchizedek; *or* in
the line of succession to Melchizedek.

    made a solemn promise: the Hebrew verb means "to swear" (see RSV),
"to take an oath," with the sense "may I die if I am not speaking the
truth." It is often difficult to use the normal term for swearing when
God is the subject, and one may need to express the content, as TEV has
done, rather than retain a reference to the ceremony of oath-taking.
    will not take it back: the Hebrew has "will not have regrets,"
that is, will not change his mind about what he has promised. The emphasis is on the fact that the LORD will keep his promise.
    You: the words are addressed to the king, who is seen as also
having priestly authority.
    in the priestly order of: literally "in the manner of," which
probably has the sense "you will be a priest-king, just as Melchizedek
was," but this also could have the meaning "in the line of succession
from Melchizedek," as the TEV note shows.
    Melchizedek: the priest-king of Jerusalem, who blessed Abraham
(Gen 14.18-20) and who was seen as the ideal early priest-king.

110.5	TEV	RSV

The Lord is at your right
   side;
when he becomes angry, he
   will defeat kings.

The Lord is at your right
   hand;
he will shatter kings on
   the day of his wrath.

    at your right side: that is, the Lord is always present to help
and protect the king.
    when he becomes angry: the Hebrew has "on the day of his (the
Lord's) wrath, anger" (see RSV), but "day" is often used in a general
way about an indefinite time, here the time when the Lord becomes
angry.
    he will defeat: literally "strike," "beat to pieces," "shatter"
(RSV), that is, the Lord will overthrow all the enemy kings who oppose
the new king.

110.6	TEV	RSV

He will pass judgment on
   the nations

He will execute judgment
   among the nations,

and fill the battlefield
   with corpses;
he will defeat kings all
   over the earth.
	filling them with corpses;
	he will shatter chiefs*g*
	   over the wide earth.

*g*Or *the head*

    pass judgment: the Hebrew word, used in the law court, means "bring justice" and "pass sentence on" (see RSV). Here the thought is that the Lord will carry out the sentence and punish nations who oppose the new king.

    fill the battlefield with corpses: literally "he fills with corpses," and TEV has supplied "the battlefield," while RSV supplies "them," meaning the nations.

    he will defeat kings: the Hebrew has "he will shatter the head," which TEV has taken in a figurative way, and which RSV has interpreted as referring to "chiefs."

110.7	TEV	RSV

	The king will drink from
	   the stream by the road,
	and strengthened, he will
	   stand victorious.
		He will drink from the
		   brook by the way;
		therefore he will lift
		   up his head.

    The king: literally "He" (RSV), but it is quite clear that the reference is to the king, not to the Lord, even if we do not know just what is meant by the action described.

    and strengthened: this is an effort to interpret the literal "therefore," that is, because he has drunk from the stream. He has been strengthened by drinking from the stream.

    he will stand victorious: literally "he will lift up the head" (see RSV), which appears to be a symbol of victory.

P S A L M   121

SECTION HEADING

    The Lord Our Protector: "Help Comes From the Lord," "The Lord Protects Us." RSV title: "A Song of Ascents."

    The Hebrew title, "A Song of Ascent, or Going Up," refers to the fact that this psalm is considered one of the pilgrim psalms sung as pilgrims go up to Jerusalem.

121.1	TEV	RSV

	I look to the mountains;
	   where will my help come
	     from?
		I lift up my eyes to the hills.
		From whence does my help come?

121.1

    I look: literally "lift up my eyes" (RSV), but this is a figurative way of speaking of seeing.

    to the mountains: this may reflect the idea that the pilgrim looked toward the mountains on which Jerusalem (the Temple) is set, or it may mean that the pilgrim fears passing through the mountains on his journey.

    where: the question sets the stage for the response in verse 2, where the psalmist continues to speak.

    help: the Hebrew word is a general one and is used for aid or assistance in any kind of difficult circumstances. If this use is difficult, one might consider translating "who will help me?"

121.2   TEV

My help will come from
    the LORD,
who made heaven and
    earth.

              RSV

My help comes from the LORD,
    who made heaven and earth.

    help: the same Hebrew verb as in verse 1.

121.3   TEV

He will not let you fall;
    your protector is always
        awake.

              RSV

He will not let your foot
      be moved,
he who keeps you will not
    slumber.

    He will not let you fall: these words seem to be addressed to the person who has spoken verses 1 and 2. The Hebrew is "he (the LORD) will not let your foot stumble" (see RSV), but the sense is "he will not let your foot strike against something so that you stumble and fall."

    your protector: God is "the one who guards (protects) you," "keeps you" (RSV).

    is always awake: literally "does not fall asleep," which TEV has chosen to express in a positive way.

121.4   TEV

The protector of Israel
    never dozes or sleeps.

              RSV

Behold, he who keeps Israel
    will neither slumber nor
      sleep.

    The protector of Israel: the Hebrew has the same construction as in verse 3, except that now the LORD is described as "the one who keeps (all) the people of Israel."

    never dozes or sleeps: the same Hebrew verb is used as in verse 3, with the addition of a verb with a similar meaning, "go to sleep." The repetition in Hebrew makes the idea emphatic, but if this is not the case in the receptor language or if two words are not readily available, some other way should be found to translate, for example, "he never under any circumstances falls asleep."

121.5   TEV   RSV
    The LORD will guard you;   The LORD is your keeper;
      he is by your side to   the LORD is your shade
        protect you.   on your right hand.

    guard: the same Hebrew verb as in verses 3 and 4.
    he is by your side to protect you: the Hebrew has "the LORD is
your shade on your right side" (see RSV), but this is a figurative way
of speaking of protection, either as a baby chick protected under the
wing of its mother or as a traveler protected from the hot sun.

121.6   TEV   RSV
    The sun will not hurt you   The sun shall not smite
        during the day,   you by day,
      nor the moon during the   nor the moon by night.
        night.

    will not hurt you: the Hebrew verb means "strike" (see RSV), as in
the English word "sunstroke."
    the moon: the rays of the moon were thought to cause harm, produc-
ing fevers and diseases as well as lunacy (from the Latin word for
"moon").

121.7   TEV   RSV
    The LORD will protect you   The LORD will keep you from
        from all danger;   all evil;
      he will keep you safe.   he will keep your life.

    all danger: literally "all evil" (RSV); this does not refer to
moral evil, but to all the bad things that might happen.
    he will keep you safe: the Hebrew has "he will guard (protect)
your life" (see RSV).

121.8   TEV   RSV
    He will protect you as you   The LORD will keep
        come and go   your going out and your
      now and forever.   coming in
                                       from this time forth and
                                         for evermore.

    as you come and go: literally "your going and your coming" (see
RSV), which is probably to be understood in the general way that TEV
has translated it, but the sense could be "as you leave the Temple and
until you come back."

P S A L M   122

SECTION HEADING

In Praise of Jerusalem^v: "A Prayer for Jerusalem."

TEV	RSV
^vHEBREW TITLE: *By David.*	A Song of Ascents. Of David.

A part of the Hebrew title (A song of ascent, or going up; by David) is found in the TEV note. This is a pilgrim psalm like Psalm 121.

122.1

TEV	RSV

I was glad when they said
    to me,
"Let us go to the LORD's
    house."
	I was glad when they said
	    to me,
	"Let us go to the house
	    of the LORD!"

they: the Hebrew does not identify who they are, but the word re-fers to fellow pilgrims who invite the psalmist to make a pilgrimage to Jerusalem with them.
the LORD's house: this is a way of speaking of the Temple in Jeru-salem.

122.2

TEV	RSV

And now we are here,
  standing inside the gates
    of Jerusalem!
	Our feet have been standing
	  within your gates, O Jeru-
	    salem!

And now we are here, standing: literally "our feet are standing," which is a figurative way of saying "we have arrived" at the Temple. Verse 1 describes the situation back in the singer's home town, while verse 2 describes the arrival in Jerusalem.
inside the gates: the Hebrew has "within your gates" (RSV), that is, the psalmist addresses Jerusalem directly. TEV has chosen to drop this personification.

122.3

TEV	RSV

Jerusalem is a city
    restored
in beautiful order and
    harmony.
	Jerusalem, built as a city
	  which is bound firmly
	    together,

restored: the Hebrew has "built" (RSV). TEV has assumed a date after the city has been rebuilt.
in beautiful order and harmony: literally "which is joined for itself together," which RSV translates "which is bound firmly together."

[128]

The words probably refer to the construction of the city and its beauty, but other interpretations are possible.

122.4   TEV

This is where the tribes
    come,
  the tribes of Israel,
to give thanks to the LORD
  according to his command.

RSV

to which the tribes go up,
  the tribes of the LORD,
as was decreed for Israel,
to give thanks to the name
  of the LORD.

come: RSV "go up" reflects the usual Old Testament practice of speaking of going up to the Temple on the hill of Zion, but this may not be meaningful in other languages.

the tribes of Israel: literally "the tribes of the LORD" (RSV), that is, "the tribes that belong to the LORD," which means the tribes of Israel.

to the LORD: the Hebrew has "to the name of the LORD" (RSV), but "name" is a way of speaking of the person.

according to his command: literally "it is a command to Israel" (see RSV), but obviously the command comes from the LORD. It may be necessary to compress the verse: "this is where the tribes of Israel will come to give thanks to the LORD. They come according to his command."

122.5   TEV

Here the kings of Israel
  sat to judge their people.

RSV

There thrones for judgment
   were set,
  the thrones of the house
     of David.

Here: the Hebrew has "for there," that is, in Jerusalem, but in light of verse 2 it may be simpler to speak of Jerusalem as here.

the kings of Israel: the Hebrew "the house of David" (RSV) means "the descendants of David," but this is a way of speaking of Israel's kings.

sat to judge their people: literally "thrones for judgment are set, thrones..." (see RSV), but it is clear that the kings are to sit on the thrones when they settle the disputes of the people of Israel.

122.6   TEV

Pray for the peace of
    Jerusalem:
"May those who love you
    prosper.

RSV

Pray for the peace of
    Jerusalem!
"May they prosper who
    love you!

Pray for the peace of Jerusalem: that is, pray that Jerusalem may have peace (and prosperity), seen as a gift from God.

those who love you: this is the meaning of the standard Hebrew text, which is probably original, but some translations follow one

122.6

Hebrew manuscript and have "your tents." In many languages it will not
be possible to address Jerusalem as "you" and one will need to translate "...our city Jerusalem...it...its..."
     prosper: the Hebrew verb has the sense "have peace and quiet,"
"have nothing to worry about," which includes prosperity but is not
limited to it.

122.7   TEV   RSV
     May there be peace inside   Peace be within your walls,
        your walls   and security within your
     and safety in your palaces."   towers!"

     safety: the Hebrew noun is related to the verb translated prosper
in verse 6, and has the sense of "lack of concern" because all is
secure and there is nothing to worry about.
     palaces: the Hebrew word means "palaces that have been fortified,"
rather than "towers" (RSV) defending the walls.

122.8   TEV   RSV
     For the sake of my relatives   For my brethren and compan-
        and friends   ions' sake
     I say to Jerusalem, "Peace   I will say, "Peace be
        be with you!"   within you!"

     For the sake of: here and in verse 9 the sense seems to be "for
the benefit of," that is, a prayer for Jerusalem will benefit his
companions and benefit the Temple, but exactly how this will happen
is not stated. One must assume that the well-being of Jerusalem means
peace and prosperity for the pilgrims.
     relatives and friends: literally "brother and companions," but
"brother" is frequently used in the general sense of a relative. Here
the reference is to the relatives and friends who have traveled to
Jerusalem with the psalmist.

122.9   TEV   RSV
     For the sake of the house   For the sake of the house
        of the LORD our God   of the LORD our God,
     I pray for your prosperity.   I will seek your good.

     I pray: literally "seek" (RSV), "look for," but the word is used
of asking God for something in prayer.
     prosperity: the Hebrew has "good," but the word is used in a
general way, "what will be good," "a blessing."

P S A L M   127

SECTION HEADING

In Praise of God's Goodness[z]: "The Lord is Good," "Trust in the Lord."

TEV	RSV
[z]HEBREW TITLE: *By Solomon.*	A Song of Ascents. Of Solomon.

The Hebrew title is "A Song of Ascent, or Going up. By Solomon."

127.1

TEV	RSV
If the LORD does not build the house, the work of the builders is useless; if the LORD does not protect the city, it does no good for the sentries to stand guard,	Unless the LORD builds the house, those who build it labor in vain. Unless the LORD watches over the city, the watchman stays awake in vain.

house: this is probably a literal reference to a home, but some understand it to refer to the Temple, the palace of the king, or the family.

useless: "worthless," "in vain" (RSV), "of no value." The same Hebrew word is translated does no good in the next line.

stand guard: the Hebrew word is the same as protect, and just as in the first line (build...builders), there is a play on words.

127.2

TEV	RSV
It is useless to work so hard for a living, getting up early and going to bed late. For the LORD provides for those he loves, while they are asleep.	It is in vain that you rise up early and go late to rest, eating the bread of anxious toil; for[m] he gives to his beloved sleep.

[m]Another reading is *so*

work so hard for a living: literally "eat the bread of hard work" (see RSV), which means "work hard to earn enough to buy food (and other necessities)."

For: this is the wording of two Hebrew manuscripts, but the standard Hebrew text has "so," "in this way," which probably has the meaning "so much," "in such great abundance," and is to be connected with what follows. See RSV and the footnote.

provides for: literally "gives to" (RSV), and in this context it probably refers to the giving of food (and other necessities).

those he loves: the Hebrew is singular, but it is to be understood in a general way.

while they are asleep: there is some uncertainty about the meaning of the Hebrew word, but it probably means "sleep," and this fits well with the first part of the verse. RSV interprets sleep itself as the gift, which seems less likely in this context.

127.3	TEV	RSV
	Children are a gift from the LORD; they are a real blessing.	Lo, sons are a heritage from the LORD, the fruit of the womb a reward.

Children: the Hebrew word "sons" (RSV) is often used for both male and female children. TEV has combined this with the literal "fruit of the womb" (RSV), which is a figurative way of speaking of children. It would be possible to translate "sons...children."

a real blessing: the word is parallel to "gift" and has the literal meaning of "wages," "reward" (RSV), but the sense is "something valuable," "...worth having."

127.4	TEV	RSV
	The sons a man has when he is young are like arrows in a soldier's hand.	Like arrows in the hand of a warrior are the sons of one's youth.

like arrows in a soldier's hand: the comparison has the meaning "will defend him, protect him" and in some languages this may have to be expressed directly rather than in a figure. The thought is that if a man has children when he is young, they will be able to take care of him when he gets old.

127.5	TEV	RSV
	Happy is the man who has many such arrows. He will never be defeated when he meets his enemies in the place of judgment.	Happy is the man who has his quiver full of them! He shall not be put to shame when he speaks with his enemies in the gate.

who has many such arrows: the Hebrew has "who has filled his quiver with them" (RSV), meaning arrows as a figure for sons, but if the figure has been dropped in verse 4, one will need to translate "who has many sons when he is young" or something similar.

He will never be defeated: literally "they will not be put to shame," in which "they" could refer to the sons but is probably to be

understood as referring to fathers of many sons. Note that RSV translates "He." The meaning of "be put to shame" (RSV) is that of being
made ashamed because of defeat or failure, and here a legal dispute is
in focus.

meets his enemies in the place of judgment: the Hebrew has "speaks
with his enemies in the gate" (RSV), but the open space near the gate
inside the city was the place where legal disputes were settled, and
"to speak" is here "to engage in debate" at the trial. (See Ruth 4.1-2.)

P S A L M   130

SECTION HEADING

A Prayer for Help: "A Prayer for Pardon" or "...Forgiveness." RSV
title: "A Song of Ascents."

The Hebrew title has "A Song of Ascent, or Going Up."

130.1   TEV   RSV
From the depths of my despair   Out of the depths I cry to
   I call to you, LORD.   thee, O LORD!

the depths of my despair: literally "depths" (RSV), "the deep,"
which refers to the deep water and is a symbol of death. The psalmist
pictures himself in a hopeless situation and about to die unless he is
helped.

130.2   TEV   RSV
Hear my cry, O Lord;   Lord, hear my voice!
   listen to my call for help!   Let thy ears be attentive
                                         to the voice of my sup-
                                         plications!

my cry: the Hebrew has "my voice" (RSV), but the real meaning is
the prayer that the Lord will listen to what he is saying, not just to
the sound of his voice.

listen: literally "let your ears be sharp (listening)" (see RSV),
which is a figurative way of saying listen.

my call for help: the Hebrew "the voice of my supplication (peti-
tion)" (see RSV) means "what I am asking for," "the help I am asking
you to give me."

130.3   TEV   RSV
If you kept a record of our   If thou, O LORD, shouldst
   sins,   mark iniquities,
   who could escape being con-   Lord, who could stand?
   demned?

[133]

130.3

you: the words are clearly addressed to the Lord, and since Lord occurs in verse 2, TEV has preferred to use the pronoun. The Hebrew of this verse has both LORD and Lord (see RSV).

kept a record of our sins: literally "keep (retain) sins," but here the meaning is probably "keep a list of (our) sins" in the sense of "keep our sins in mind," "refuse to forgive our sins."

who: the rhetorical question may have to be dropped and the meaning expressed directly, for example, "no one would be able to escape..." or "you would condemn us all."

escape being condemned: literally "stand" (RSV), but this has the sense "remain standing uncondemned in the court of judgment" (TEV) or "stay alive," "keep from being put to death."

130.4 TEV	RSV
But you forgive us, so that we should stand in awe of you.	But there is forgiveness with thee, that thou mayest be feared.

you forgive us: the Hebrew has "with you (there is) forgiveness" (RSV), but in most languages it will be better to express this act of forgiveness with a verb form or with the idea "you are always ready to forgive us."

we should stand in awe of you: literally "you should be feared (by people)," but it is clearer to express the idea in an active form. The word "fear" does not have the sense of being afraid in the face of danger, but rather have reverence for, be in awe of, obey, worship.

130.5 TEV	RSV
I wait eagerly for the LORD's help, and in his word I trust.	I wait for the LORD, my soul waits, and in his word I hope;

I wait eagerly for the LORD's help: the Hebrew repeats "I wait eagerly for the LORD (to help me); my soul (my life) waits eagerly" (see RSV). The repetition is a way of intensifying the thought, and "my soul" or "my life" is a way of speaking of the total person of the psalmist.

his word: that is, "what the LORD has said," and particularly the LORD's promises to help those who turn to him.

I trust: although the Hebrew verb is different, it has a meaning similar to that of the verb in the first part of the verse, "wait, wait for," but the underlying idea is that of "hope" (RSV), "trust" in waiting for the LORD to act.

130.6 TEV	RSV
I wait for the Lord more eagerly than watchmen wait for the dawn—	my soul waits for the LORD more than watchmen for the morning,

than watchmen wait for the dawn.	more than watchmen for the morning.

I wait: literally "my soul waits" (see verse 5), with "wait" being supplied from the context.

watchmen wait for the dawn: the repetition serves to emphasize the idea of waiting. If repetition does not serve this function in the receptor language, another way should be found to emphasize the longing of the psalmist (the watchmen).

130.7

TEV	RSV
Israel, trust in the LORD, because his love is constant and he is always willing to save.	O Israel, hope in the LORD! For with the LORD there is steadfast love, and with him is plenteous redemption.

trust: see verse 5.

his love is constant: the Hebrew has "with the LORD is love (constant love)," which means "the LORD is always ready to love." The word translated "love" is the word frequently used for the faithfulness of the LORD in keeping his promises, the fact that he can always be trusted.

he is always willing to save: RSV translates the literal "with him is much redemption" (see verse 4 and the line above for the construction), and "redemption" (the LORD redeems) is used in a general way, with the meaning "save" or "deliver" rather than in the literal sense of "buy back."

130.8

TEV	RSV
He will save his people Israel from all their sins.	And he will redeem Israel from all his iniquities.

his people Israel: literally "Israel," but this means the people of Israel, descended from their ancestor Israel or Jacob.

P S A L M 139

SECTION HEADING

God's Complete Knowledge and Care*f*: "God Knows and Cares for Me."

TEV	RSV
f HEBREW TITLE: *A psalm by David.*	To the choirmaster. A Psalm of David.

139.1

The Hebrew title is "For the choirmaster; by David; a Psalm," but exactly what is meant is not certain.

139.1   TEV   RSV
    LORD, you have examined me   O LORD, thou hast searched me
       and you know me.   and known me!

examined: the Hebrew verb means "look carefully at," "explore," "investigate." The word emphasizes carefulness and thoroughness.

139.2   TEV   RSV
    You know everything I do;   Thou knowest when I sit down
       from far away you understand   and when I rise up;
       all my thoughts.   thou discernest my thoughts
                                           from afar.

everything I do: the Hebrew "my sitting down and my rising up" (see RSV) is a way of speaking about the total activity of the psalmist.
    from far away: that is, even though the LORD is far away in heaven, he knows what the psalmist is thinking.

139.3   TEV   RSV
    You see me, whether I am   Thou searchest out my path
       working or resting;   and my lying down,
       you know all my actions.   and art acquainted with all
                                           my ways.

You see me, whether I am working or resting: the Hebrew has "measure off (know, determine, examine) my path (walking) and my lying (resting)," and this means that the LORD knows all the activities of the psalmist (see verse 2).
    know: "you are fully acquainted with."
    all my actions: the literal "all my ways" (RSV) means "everything I do."

139.4   TEV   RSV
    Even before I speak,   Even before a word is on
       you already know what   my tongue,
       I will say.   lo, O LORD, thou knowest
                                          it altogether.

Even before I speak: the Hebrew "there is (yet) no word on my tongue" (see RSV) means "I have not yet made a sound."
    you already know: literally "you, LORD, already know."
    what I will say: this is what the literal "all of it" seems to mean. The RSV "altogether" is not clear.

[136]

139.5 TEV	RSV
You are all around me on every side; you protect me with your power.	Thou dost beset me behind and before, and layest thy hand upon me.

You are all around me: the Hebrew verb is used of surrounding a city in siege, but here the sense is that the LORD "surrounds" the psalmist to protect him. RSV "beset me behind and before" seems to be a threatening activity.

you protect me with your power: the Hebrew has "you place your hand upon me," and this also has the sense of "to protect me (care for me)." The word "hand" often expresses the idea of power or activity. The literal translation of RSV seems to mean punishment.

139.6 TEV	RSV
Your knowledge of me is too deep; it is beyond my under- standing.	Such knowledge is too wonderful for me; it is high, I cannot attain it.

Your knowledge of me: the Hebrew has "knowledge," but it seems evident that the reference is to the LORD's knowledge about the psalmist rather than to what the psalmist knows. One might translate "You know me so well that..."

too deep: literally "too marvelous (too wonderful) for me" (see RSV), but in English one speaks of deep knowledge.

it is beyond my understanding: the Hebrew has "it is high; I am not able (to come) to it," but the sense is clearly "I don't understand it."

139.7 TEV	RSV
Where could I go to escape from you? Where could I get away from your presence?	Whither shall I go from thy Spirit? Or whither shall I flee from thy presence?

Where could I go: the rhetorical question may have to be replaced with a statement: "there is no place that I could go."

to escape from you: literally "from your spirit (life)." However, (in parallel with the next line) "spirit (life)" does not refer to an extension of God's power but to God himself. The word "spirit (life)" is used in the same way to speak of human beings as persons. The RSV "Spirit" is open to misinterpretation.

get away from your presence: the Hebrew has "run away from your face," but "face" frequently has the sense of "presence."

139.8 TEV	RSV
If I went up to heaven, you would be there;	If I ascend to heaven, thou art there!

if I lay down in the world of the dead, you would be there.	If I make my bed in Sheol, thou art there!

lay down in the world of the dead: the Hebrew has "if I made up my bed in Sheol" (see RSV), but "make up a bed" has the sense of "prepare to lie down to sleep." The Hebrew word "Sheol" is the name for the world of the dead, thought of as beneath the earth. The psalmist speaks of the most distant parts of the universe, heaven above and the world of the dead below.

139.9 TEV	RSV
If I flew away beyond the east or lived in the farthest place in the west,	If I take the wings of the morning and dwell in the uttermost parts of the sea,

flew away beyond the east: literally "took the wings of the dawn" (see RSV). There is some uncertainty about the meaning, and there is a textual variant, but it seems likely that the psalmist is saying, "if I flew as far to the east as I could."
the farthest place in the west: the Hebrew has "the farthest sea," but the word "sea" often refers to the direction west since the Mediterranean is west of Palestine. The psalmist is still speaking of the most distant places: up, down, east, or west.

139.10 TEV	RSV
you would be there to lead me, you would be there to help me.	even there thy hand shall lead me, and thy right hand shall hold me.

you would be there to lead me: in the Hebrew, "even there your hand would lead me"; "hand" is used in the sense of power or activity of the person and is not understood literally.
be there to help me: literally "your right hand would hold me," but this is figurative language for the idea of help.

139.11 TEV	RSV
I could ask the darkness to hide me or the light around me to turn into night,	If I say, "Let only darkness cover me, and the light about me be night,"

I could ask: note that TEV has shifted to indirect speech, which is stylistically better in English.
to hide me: the Hebrew verb means "crush" but possibly has a more general sense of "cover" (RSV). Some translations change the text to read "cover." The general sense is certainly "hide."

the light: this is the reading of the standard Hebrew text and probably original, but some translations adopt a reading from the Dead Sea Scrolls, "girdle," and translate "may night encircle me."

139.12	TEV	RSV
	but even darkness is not dark for you, and the night is as bright as the day. Darkness and light are the same to you.	even the darkness is not dark to thee, the night is bright as the day; for darkness is as light with thee.

Darkness and light are the same to you: literally "as darkness, as light," which some translations drop as an addition to the text, but this is not necessary. One might translate "you see as well in the darkness as you do in the light."

139.13	TEV	RSV
	You created every part of me; you put me together in my mother's womb.	For thou didst form my inward parts, thou didst knit me together in my mother's womb.

created: the Hebrew verb is used of the creative activity of God.
every part of me: literally "my kidneys," but this seems to be used in an extended way for all the many parts of the body. Many translations use something like "inward parts" (RSV).
put me together: the Hebrew verb has the sense of "weave," "knit together" (RSV).

139.14	TEV	RSV
	I praise you because you are to be feared; all you do is strange and wonderful. I know it with all my heart.	I praise thee, for thou art fearful and wonderful.^{t} Wonderful are thy works! Thou knowest me right well;

^{t}Cn Compare Gk Syr Jerome: Heb *fearful things I am wonderful*

you are to be feared: TEV translates a Hebrew text found in the Dead Sea Scrolls. The standard Hebrew text seems to combine this word with the following word ("I am considered different") and could perhaps be translated "fearful deeds—I am a wonder." This has been taken to mean "I am fearfully and wonderfully made," but the meaning is not certain. The Hebrew of the verse is difficult to understand. The RSV is a conjecture, which can be seen from the footnote.
all you do is strange and wonderful: see the first part of the verse. The standard Hebrew text has "your works are wonderful," that is, "all that you do is wonderful," and TEV has interpreted "your works are exceedingly wonderful" as all you do is strange and wonderful.

139.14

I know it with all my heart: the Hebrew has "my soul (life) knows it well," where "soul (life)" stands for the person. The wording "you know my soul (me) well" (see RSV) comes from changing the text. It does fit the context better but is probably not the original reading.

139.15 TEV	RSV
When my bones were being formed, carefully put together in my mother's womb, when I was growing there in secret, you knew that I was there—	my frame was not hidden from thee, when I was being made in secret, intricately wrought in the depths of the earth.

When my bones were being formed: TEV has rearranged the elements of the Hebrew to make it easier to understand, literally "my bones were not hidden from you when I was being made in secret, (when) I was being carefully woven (carefully formed) in the depths of the earth." TEV has taken "bones" in the sense of the total bone structure, the skeleton.

my mother's womb: the literal "depths of the earth" (RSV) is understood by TEV and many scholars as a figurative way of speaking of the womb. The words may, however, reflect the idea that children were formed in mother earth before they entered the womb. If this interpretation is followed, one would need to translate "when I was being carefully put together in the earth before I was born" or something similar.

you knew that I was there: this translates the Hebrew "(I) was not hidden from you" (see RSV). In many languages it will be better to express the idea positively rather than negatively.

139.16 TEV	RSV
you saw me before I was born. The days allotted to me had all been recorded in your book, before any of them ever began.	Thy eyes beheld my unformed substance; in thy book were written, every one of them, the days that were formed for me, when as yet there was none of them.

you saw me before I was born: literally "your eyes saw my embryo" (see RSV). The sense is that the Lord knew all about me even during the formation in the womb.

The days allotted to me: the Hebrew is "days were formed" (see RSV), which TEV and others take to refer to the number of days (years) the person would live. The thought would be that before birth the LORD determines how long a person will live. By changing the text, one may arrive at a translation such as "day by day my limbs were formed," but this is probably not the original sense.

your book: this would be the book in which the Lord records the number of years that a person will live.

before any of them ever began: the standard Hebrew text has "and not one among them," but another form of the text has "and for him (or, it) one among them," which would refer to the day of birth. It is better to follow the standard Hebrew text, as RSV and TEV do.

139.17 TEV	RSV
O God, how difficult I find your thoughts;^{g} how many of them there are!	How precious to me are thy thoughts, O God! How vast is the sum of them!

^{g}how difficult I find your thoughts; *or* how precious are your thoughts to me.

how difficult: the Hebrew word probably means "difficult," but it may have the meaning "precious" (RSV), "rare," "of great value." The how-construction has the meaning "I find your thoughts very difficult," but the idea is expressed in an intensive way.

139.18 TEV	RSV
If I counted them, they would be more than the grains of sand. When I awake, I am still with you.	If I would count them, they are more than the sand. When I awake, I am still with thee.^{u}
	^{u}Or *were I to come to the end I would still be with thee.*

awake: this is the meaning of the standard Hebrew text, but some Hebrew manuscripts have "finished," that is, "when I have finished counting." It seems better to follow the standard text with TEV and RSV but to note the footnote.
I am still with you: the thought seems to be that in spite of all efforts (thinking until he falls asleep or counting on to the end), the psalmist must recognize that he is in the presence of God, and it is not possible to understand God's thoughts.

139.19 TEV	RSV
O God, how I wish you would kill the wicked! How I wish violent men would leave me alone!	O that thou wouldst slay the wicked, O God, and that men of blood would depart from me,

kill the wicked: the psalmist thinks of the enemies of the Lord as his own enemies.
violent men: literally "men of bloods," that is, men who shed blood. The Hebrew uses direct address: "depart from me, men of bloods."

139.20 TEV	RSV

They say wicked things about you;
  they speak evil things against your name.*h*
	men who maliciously defy thee,
	  who lift themselves up against thee for evil!*v*

h Probable text they speak...name;   *v*Cn: Heb uncertain
Hebrew unclear.

They say: the Hebrew text has "say," but some translations change the text to mean "defy," "rebel" (see RSV).

wicked things: literally "to evil (wickedness)." RSV translates "maliciously," that is, "with evil intents." The sense is "they speak against you because they are evil" or "...because they make plans to rebel" or "...because they are not loyal to you."

they speak evil things against your name: TEV has changed the text to get this meaning. The standard Hebrew text seems to say literally "they lift up in vain your cities," but almost everyone recognizes that this makes little sense in the context. If "your cities" could be understood as "your enemies," which is perhaps possible, the sense would be "they are your enemies and they speak vain (evil) things (against you)." Some Hebrew manuscripts have "they lift up in vain toward you," which can possibly be interpreted as "they rebel in vain against you." The translator will simply have to choose one of the interpretations with the knowledge that the meaning is very uncertain. A note should probably indicate the uncertainty, as in TEV.

139.21 TEV	RSV
O LORD, how I hate those who hate you! How I despise those who rebel against you!	Do I not hate them that hate thee, O LORD? And do I not loathe them that rise up against thee?

I hate: in Hebrew the two elements of the verse are expressed as rhetorical questions, which must be avoided in many languages.

139.22 TEV	RSV

I hate them with a total hatred;
  I regard them as my enemies.
	I hate them with perfect hatred;
	  I count them my enemies.

a total hatred: that is, "there is no end to my hatred," "I hate without any limits."

139.23 TEV	RSV
Examine me, O God, and know my mind;	Search me, O God, and know my heart!

| test me, and discover my thoughts. | Try me and know my thoughts! |

Examine: the same Hebrew verb as in verse 1.
mind: literally "heart," but the heart is understood to be the seat of thinking, which is called "the mind" in English.

139.24

TEV	RSV
Find out if there is any evil in me and guide me in the everlasting way.^{i}	And see if there be any wicked^w way in me, and lead me in the way everlasting!^{x}

^{i}the everlasting way; or the ways of my ancestors.

^{w}Heb *hurtful*
^{x}Or *the ancient way*. Compare Jer 6.16

any evil: the Hebrew may be translated literally as "a way of hardship, hurt" or as "a way of idol." In the first case the meaning would be a way that hurts God, that is, is sinful. In the second case the meaning would be "a way of idolatry," that is, "have practiced idolatry." The verse contains a contrast between the way of rebellion against God (evil or idolatry) and the way of obedience to God.

the everlasting way: that is, "God's way." As the TEV marginal note shows, the meaning may be "the ways of my ancestors (who obeyed God)."

P S A L M   150

SECTION HEADING

Praise the LORD!: "The Final Psalm of Praise."

150.1

TEV	RSV
Praise the LORD!	Praise the LORD! Praise God in his sanctuary; praise him in his mighty firmament!
Praise God in his Temple! Praise his strength in heaven!	

Praise the LORD!: this is the meaning of the Hebrew, often translated as "hallelujah."
Praise: each line of the psalm contains the same verb for praise (hallel).
his Temple: literally "his holy (place; RSV sanctuary)," which probably refers to the Temple in Jerusalem, but could be understood of the Temple in heaven.
his strength in heaven: literally "in the dome, his strength,"

150.1

where "dome" is the same word for the "sky" found in Genesis 1.6-7. TEV has taken "his strength" to refer to the strength of the LORD, but other translations interpret it as referring to heaven, "his mighty heaven," or RSV "his mighty firmament."

150.2	TEV	RSV
	Praise him for the mighty things he has done. Praise his supreme greatness.	Praise him for his mighty deeds; praise him according to his exceeding greatness!

the mighty things he has done: this refers to his powerful deeds in creation and to his saving acts in the history of Israel.

150.3	TEV	RSV
	Praise him with trumpets. Praise him with harps and lyres.	Praise him with trumpet sound; praise him with lute and harp!

trumpets: an instrument made of ram's horn.
harps: a stringed instrument; RSV "lute."
lyres: a different type of stringed instrument; RSV "harp."

150.4	TEV	RSV
	Praise him with drums and dancing. Praise him with harps and flutes.	Praise him with timbrel and dance; praise him with strings and pipe!

drums: a kind of tambourine; RSV "timbrel."
dancing: a kind of circling dance.
harps: a third type of stringed instrument. TEV repeats "harp," although the Hebrew word is different; RSV "strings."
flutes: a wind instrument; RSV "pipe."

150.5	TEV	RSV
	Praise him with cymbals. Praise him with loud cymbals.	Praise him with sounding cymbals; praise him with loud clashing cymbals!

cymbals...loud cymbals: two kinds of cymbals are named, perhaps large and small. For all of these musical instruments the translator may consult a good Bible dictionary, but he will probably simply have to select from the various musical instruments known in his own culture and parallel the type of instrument as closely as possible.

150.6   TEV

   Praise the LORD, all living
      creatures!

   Praise the LORD!

RSV

Let everything that breathes
     praise the LORD!
Praise the LORD!

all living creatures: literally "everything that breathes," that is, all animals and men.

Praise the LORD!: the same expression as at the beginning of the psalm.

SELECTED BIBLIOGRAPHY

Anderson, A. A. 1972. The Book of Psalms (New Century Bible). Oliphants. Two volumes.

The translator will find these two volumes very helpful in dealing with details of interpretation. It can be used by those not knowing Hebrew, although Hebrew words are often transliterated.

Kissane, E. J. 1964. The Book of Psalms. Browne.

The book includes a formal correspondent translation with notes on the Hebrew text. It will be of most help to those who know Hebrew, but others will find the comments useful.

McCullough, W. S., and Taylor, W. R. 1955. The Book of Psalms (Interpreter's Bible). Abingdon.

This volume provides helpful information on background and structure. Useful comments on problem passages are often found. Knowledge of Hebrew is not required, although occasionally Hebrew is cited.

Rodd, C. S. 1963, 1964. Psalms 1-72; Psalms 73-150. Epworth.

This is a brief treatment of the Book of Psalms and of a number of problem passages in each psalm. It can easily be used by those without knowledge of Hebrew.

Weiser, Artur. 1962. The Psalms (Old Testament Library). Westminster.

This book gives much attention to the theological significance of the psalms and their use in ancient Israel, but the translator will also find the comments on some psalms quite helpful.

GLOSSARY

This glossary contains terms which are technical from an exegetical
or a linguistic viewpoint. Other terms not defined here may be referred
to in a Bible dictionary.

active. See voice.

adjective is a word which limits, describes, or qualifies a noun. In
   English, "red," "tall," "beautiful," "important," etc., are adjectives.

ancient translations. See versions.

conjecture. See textual.

construction. See structure.

context is that which precedes and/or follows any part of a discourse.
   For example, the context of a word or phrase in Scripture would be the
   other words and phrases associated with it in the sentence, paragraph,
   section, and even the entire book in which it occurs. The context of
   a term often affects its meaning, so that a word does not mean exactly
   the same thing in one context that it does in another.

direct address, direct discourse. See discourse.

discourse is a connected and continuous communication by means of language, whether spoken or written. The way in which the elements of a
   discourse are arranged is called discourse structure. Direct discourse
   is the reproduction of the actural words of one person quoted and
   included in the discourse of another person; for example, "He declared,
   'I will have nothing to do with this man.'" Indirect discourse is the
   reporting of the words of one person in the discourse of another
   person, but in an altered grammatical form rather than as an exact
   quotation; for example, "He said he would have nothing to do with that
   man."

emphasis (emphatic, emphatically) is the special importance given to an
   element in a discourse, sometimes indicated by the choice of words or
   by position in the sentence. For example, in "Never will I eat pork
   again," "Never" is given emphasis by placing it at the beginning of
   the sentence.

[149]

explicit refers to information which is expressed in the words of a
  discourse. This is in contrast to implicit information. See implicit.

figure, figurative expression involves the use of words in other than
  their literal or ordinary sense, in order to bring out some aspect of
  meaning by means of comparison or association.

finite verb. See infinitive.

implicit (implied) refers to information that is not formally represented
  in a discourse, since it is assumed that it is already known to the
  receptor, or evident from the meaning of the words in question. For
  example, the phrase "the other son" carries with it the implicit information that there is a son in addition to the one mentioned. This is
  in contrast to explicit information, which is expressly stated in a
  discourse. See explicit.

indirect address, indirect discourse. See discourse.

infinitive is a verb form which indicates an action or state without
  specifying such factors as agent or time. It is in contrast to a
  finite verb form, which often indicates person, number, tense, mode,
  or aspect.

intensive is a word which has the effect of making stronger the action
  expressed in another word, for example, "very" in "very active," or
  "highly" in "highly competitive."

literal means the ordinary or primary meaning of a term or expression,
  in contrast with a figurative meaning. A literal translation is one
  which represents the exact words and word order of the source language;
  such a translation frequently is unnatural or awkward in the receptor
  language.

manuscripts are books, documents, letters, etc., written by hand. Thou-
  sands of manuscript copies of verious New Testament books still exist
  but none of the original manuscripts.

noun is a word that names a person, place, thing, idea, etc., and often
  serves to specify a subject or topic of a discourse.

parallel, parallelism generally refers to some similarity in the content
  and/or form of a construction; for example, "The man was blind, and he
  could not see." The structures that correspond to each other in the
  two statements are said to be parallel.

passive, passive form, passive voice. See voice.

person, as a grammatical term, refers to the speaker, the person spoken
  to, or the person or thing spoken about. First person is the person(s)
  speaking ("I," "me," "my," "mine," "we," "us," "our," "ours"). Second

person is the person(s) or thing(s) spoken to ("thou," "thee," "thy," "thine," "ye," "you," "your," "yours"). Third person is the person(s) or thing(s) spoken about ("he," "she," "it," "his," "her," "them," "their," etc.). The examples here given are all pronouns, but in many languages the verb forms have affixes which indicate first, second, or third persons and also indicate whether they are singular or plural.

personification is a reference to an inanimate object or an abstract idea as though it were personal and/or animate; as in "Wisdom is calling out," referring to wisdom as if it were a person.

phrase is a grammatical construction of two or more words, but less than a complete clause or a sentence. A phrase is usually given a name according to its function in a sentence, such as "noun phrase," "verb phrase," "prepositional phrase," etc.

plural refers to the form of a word which indicates more than one. See singular.

problems, textual problems. See textual.

receptor is the person(s) receiving a message. The receptor language is the language into which a translation is made. For example, in a translation from Hebrew into German, Hebrew is the source language and German is the receptor language. The receptor culture is the the culture of the people for whom a translation is made, especially when it differs radically from the culture of the people for whom the original message was written.

redundant refers to anything which is entirely predictable from the context.

restructure is to reconstruct or rearrange. See structure.

rhetorical refers to forms of speech which are employed to highlight or make more attractive some aspect of a discourse. A rhetorical question, for example, is not designed to elicit an answer but to make an emphatic statement.

singular refers to the form of a word which indicates one thing or person, in contrast to plural, which indicates more than one. See plural.

structure is the systematic arrangement of the elements of language, including the ways in which words combine into phrases, phrases into clauses, and clauses into sentences. Because this process may be compared to the building of a house or a bridge, such words as structure and construction are used in reference to it. To separate and rearrange the various components of a sentence or other unit of discourse in the translation process is to restructure it.

style is a particular or a characteristic manner in discourse. Each language has certain distinctive stylistic features which cannot be repro-
duced literally in another language. Within any language, certain
groups of speakers may have their characteristic discourse styles,
and among individual speakers and writers, each has his own style.

subject is one of the major divisions of a clause, the other being the
predicate. Typically the subject is a noun phrase. It should not be
confused with semantic "agent."

symbol is a form, whether linguistic or nonlinguistic, which is arbitrarily
and conventionally associated with a particular meaning. For example,
the word "cross" is a linguistic symbol, referring to a particular
object. Similarly, within the Christian tradition, the cross as an
object is a symbol for the death of Jesus.

tense is usually a form of a verb which indicates time relative to a
discourse or some event in a discourse. The most common forms of tense
are past, present, and future.

textual refers to the various Greek and Hebrew manuscripts of the Scrip-
tures. Textual variants are forms of the same passage that differ in
one or more details. Textual problems arise when it is difficult to
reconcile or to account for conflicting forms of the same text in two
or more manuscripts. A conjecture is a form of the text which some
scholars believe represents the original, although no known manuscript
contains such a form.

variants, textual variants. See textual.

verbs are a grammatical class of words which express existence, action,
or occurrence, as "be," "become," "run," "think," etc.

versions are translations. The ancient, or early, versions are translations of the Bible, or of portions of the Bible, made in early times;
for example, the Greek Septuagint, the ancient Syriac, or the Ethiopic
versions.

voice in grammar is the relation of the action expressed by a verb to the
participants in the action. In English and many other languages, the
active voice indicates that the subject performs the action ("John hit
the man"), while the passive voice indicates that the subject is being
acted upon ("the man was hit").

INDEX

This index includes concepts, key words, and terms for which the Guide contains a discussion useful for translators.

Index